Public Talk Series: 1

LIVING INTELLIGENTLY

Swami Dayananda Saraswati
Arsha Vidya

Arsha Vidya
Research and Publication Trust
Chennai

Published by :
Arsha Vidya Research
and Publication Trust
32 / 4 ' Sri Nidhi ' Apts III Floor
Sir Desika Road Mylapore
Chennai 600 004 INDIA
Tel : 044 2499 7023
Telefax : 2499 7131
Email : avrandpc@gmail.com

ISBN : 978 - 81 - 903636 - 1 - 7

First Edition	: June	2006	Copies	: 1000
1st Reprint	: May	2009	Copies	: 2000

Design :
Suchi Ebrahim

Printed by :
Sudarsan Graphics
27, Neelakanta Mehta Street
T. Nagar, Chennai 600 017
Email : info@sudarsan.com

Contents

Preface

I am very happy to see in print the series of talks I gave in Chennai under different titles for meaningful 'Living'. I enjoyed my reading these manuscripts inasmuch as the material therein was an outcome of my open thinking. In fact, in some places I was amused as well as surprised. Anyone who reads this book, I am sure, will find it refreshingly useful. I congratulate the dedicated people at the Arsha Vidya Research and Publication Trust, for this thoughtful publication.

Swami Dayananda Saraswati

Rishikesh
27 May 2006

Key to Transliteration and Pronunciation of Sanskrit Letters

Sanskrit is a highly phonetic language and hence accuracy in articulation of the letters is important. For those unfamiliar with the *Devanägari* script, the international transliteration is a guide to the proper pronunciation of Sanskrit letters.

अ	*a*	*(but)*
आ	*ā*	*(father)*
इ	*i*	*(it)*
ई	*ī*	*(beat)*
उ	*u*	*(full)*
ऊ	*ū*	*(pool)*
ऋ	*ṛ*	*(rhythm)*
ॠ	*ṝ*	*(marine)*
ऌ	*ḷ*	*(revelry)*
ए	*e*	*(play)*
ऐ	*ai*	*(aisle)*
ओ	*o*	*(go)*
औ	*au*	*(loud)*
क	*ka*	*(seek)* 1
ख	*kha*	*(blockhead)**1
ग	*ga*	*(get)* 1
घ	*gha*	*(log hut)**1
ङ	*ṅa*	*(sing)* 1
च	*ca*	*(chunk)* 2
छ	*cha*	*(catch him)**2
ज	*ja*	*(jump)* 2
झ	*jha*	*(hedgehog)**2
ञ	*ña*	*(bunch)* 2
ट	*öa*	*(true)**3
ठ	*öha*	*(anthill)**3
ड	*òa*	*(drum)**3
ढ	*òha*	*(godhead)**3
ण	*ëa*	*(under)**3
त	*ta*	*(path)**4
थ	*tha*	*(thunder)**4
द	*da*	*(that)**4
ध	*dha*	*(breathe)**4
न	*na*	*(nut)**4
प	*pa*	*(put)* 5
फ	*pha*	*(loophole)**5
ब	*ba*	*(bin)* 5
भ	*bha*	*(abhor)**5
म	*ma*	*(much)* 5
य	*ya*	*(loyal)*
र	*ra*	*(red)*
ल	*la*	*(luck)*
व	*va*	*(vase)*
श	*ça*	*(sure)*
ष	*ña*	*(shun)*
स	*sa*	*(so)*
ह	*ha*	*(hum)*

•	à	*anusvära*	(nasalisation of preceding vowel)
:	ù	*visarga*	(aspiration of preceding vowel)
*			No exact English equivalents for these letters

1. Guttural – Pronounced from throat
2. Palatal – Pronounced from palate
3. Lingual – Pronounced from cerebrum
4. Dental – Pronounced from teeth
5. Labial – Pronounced from lips

The 5th letter of each of the above class – called nasals – are also pronounced nasally.

Talk 1

Intelligent living implies relating objectively

One has no choice in some areas. Should I breathe or not? I have no choice if I want to live, of course. Should I relate to the world or not? While living, there is no choice. I need to relate. Living is relating. One can be alive without relating to the world, but that is not living. While one is asleep one does not relate to the world, though people around may relate to the person because the person is having a 'sound' sleep. Even in a state of coma one does not relate to the world. With all the medical support available now, one can live for years in a coma. One woman lived for ten years in a coma in the USA. That is not living. I make a distinction between being alive and living my life. When I live my life, I need to relate to the world. If I open my eyes I relate. When I think of something I relate. When I imagine something I relate. Even in dream I relate. While I am awake I relate to the world.

So while living, I need to relate to the world; I have no choice. There is also no choice in exercising choice for a human being. I need to choose. I do not choose to relate, though I may choose to avoid a relationship, which is also a form of relating. I see you when I open my eyes; this is relating. It is a subject-object relationship; I am the subject and you are the object. When you hear me you relate. It is impossible to avoid relating. It is impossible to avoid making a choice. I may not be very refined in making proper choices, but choice I have to make. Should I eat or not, I need to choose.

How often I eat, I should choose. What I eat, I need to choose. When I eat, I need to choose. How much I eat, I need to choose. Well, there is choice all the way.

How do you respond to a situation?

When you relate to a situation, how do you respond to that situation? If you consciously respond, there is choice. If you are spontaneous, the choice is spontaneous. When somebody slips in front of you, you bend down and extend a helping hand. There is no big deliberation involved here, but at the same time the choice is spontaneous. When your action is right without any deliberation, I would use the word spontaneous for that choice. I qualify that choice by the adjective spontaneous. If what you do is not becoming, is not acceptable, or is mechanical, then there is hardly any choice; the action is impulsive. You cannot say 'I kicked him spontaneously.'

Naturally, the availability of this choice varies from person to person in terms of degrees. One has to take the initiative in developing the capacity to choose. In fact, one has to exercise one's choice to become more deliberate, more conscious, in order to become spontaneously good, spontaneously doing what is to be done. Since my relating to the world is inevitable, either I relate to the world intelligently or I relate unintelligently and mechanically. Now the question is: Is there a choice in my living intelligently? There is no choice.

The problem is, everyone thinks he or she is living intelligently, and that it is the others who are unintelligent.

The others also think the same way and so everybody is intelligent. However, since everybody also thinks that others are not that intelligent, it follows that all of us are unintelligent. This is some kind of a funny logic. Of course, one can try to be more intelligent. How does one decide whether one is living intelligently or not? Is it by an Intelligence Quotient test? One may have a high IQ and yet be given to crime. Therefore, what does it take to live intelligently? I am going to think aloud.

One thing seems very striking to me. To be intelligent is to be objective. The word objective naturally presupposes another word, subjective, its opposite. To be objective is not to be subjective. When I see a flower and accept it as a flower, I am objective. When I see a person and accept the person as he or she is, I am objective.

Subjectivity in value structure

The problem is, I do not know what kind of a person he or she is, in terms of the person's thinking, emotions and value structure. One can live with a person for years and still wonder whether one knows the person. It is very difficult to know another person. Therefore, any judgement on my part about that person is going to be partly subjective and partly objective, or totally subjective, except that physically it is the same person. Sometimes even physically the person is mistaken for another person.

For instance, I have a look-alike in Mount Abu. His name is Swami Ishwarananda, a learned swami. Sometimes I get *namaskāras*, salutations at the airports. The person, who has done the *namaskāra*, seems to know me. He asks me, "Swamiji, when did you come from Mount Abu?" I know that he is totally mistaken. This is subjectivity object-wise. The whole person is mistaken for somebody else. Aware that he has made a mistake I tell him, "I am not Ishwaranandaji." This kind of mistake, where one person is mistaken for another person, is very simple and the correction is also very simple. But I am talking of two people living together and yet not understanding each other.

The fact is that one trusts the other, being married to him or her. It means one can safely complain about the other. There is a whole background for this. I am going to explore all this background later. Here, however, to highlight the problem, first we have to understand the problem. One wonders whether it will ever be possible to make the other understand. Many a good relationship has been broken for good because of this incapacity to understand the other. Therefore, there is subjectivity in all our relationships.

In our value structures there is much subjectivity. Certain things are taken to be more real or important than they are. They are taken to be so important that one becomes possessed of them. Pursuits become very obsessive. Friendships become very obsessive, strangulating. One is not able to relate objectively in the world. Therefore, it is not proper for one to neglect something that needs attention in order for one to live one's life very objectively. One has no choice in this.

One has no choice in being objective

To be objective is to be intelligent. This is what I call intelligent living. I need to be objective in many areas. It is not enough that I understand this in general, vaguely. General or vague understanding does not work here. I must look deeply into certain areas that need to be understood, ventilated. Some fresh air of understanding has to be brought in to make myself very well informed so that I can live a life of objectivity.

There is a world available for public appreciation, but I live in my own world of fears, anxieties and projections. Everybody is living in a bubble. Even the love-bubble is the same. I have to prick this bubble and breathe fresh air. Let us understand first what is the reason for this subjectivity; then we will look into what it takes to be objective.

What are the factors involved in subjectivity? Ignorance can be one factor. Generally, that is the factor we address when we teach. We teach 'what is' so that you get clear knowledge with reference to certain realities. Our not knowing or vaguely knowing or wrongly knowing is *avidyā*, ignorance. *Vidyā* is the opposite. This is one thing.

There is another factor, which is psychological and cannot be dismissed. Anyone who does not wish to address his or her psychological issues, because they are very painful, dismisses the psychological factor as merely psychological. We are going to address it.

Addressing the psychological factor

When one is born, there is total helplessness. A human child is not as simple as a calf. A calf is born; it struggles and stands on its four legs. A human baby, perhaps, was very safe and secure only when it was not yet born. The baby's body connected to the mother, having its own heart, happily moving and floating inside, was totally secure, perhaps, for the only period of time in its entire life. It is born to start an independent life. What a start to an independent life! To live independently one must have everything that is necessary. At least one must be able to beg.

Suppose someone gets married without employment, without any possibility of future employment and without rich in-laws. He gets married because of 'what others will think,' as though others have the time to think about him. Everybody has his or her own problems. When you meet somebody, being courteous, you have to ask something. We Indians have our own way of greeting each other. "How are you?" After that, there is an awkward pause since we do not have much to say, but to continue the conversation we ask, "How is your daughter? How is your son? Is he married?"

"Not yet."

"Oh, not yet?"

What else does one say? The mother, however, is worried that her son is not married. She wonders, "What will others think?" Others do not have time to think about such things. They only ask some polite questions. They are not worried about her son's marriage. So this person is married because of 'what others will think.' He has no job and no possibility of a job and the bride is also not employed. At least both of them can beg.

The new born baby, however, cannot beg. It is starting an independent life; this is what I am talking about. The baby was safe a minute before. It is unsafe now, helpless, totally, since the cord is already snapped. It has to start its journey, an independent journey. Nothing is known. The eyes are still closed, not yet open. It starts its life with absolute trust in the person whose hands pick it up. It is a hundred percent trust. Maybe, vaguely, while prenatal, the baby had heard the voice of the mother. It hears the same voice now. Perhaps there is a small disturbance inside if the voice is different, because the baby is given to somebody else. Only a small disturbance, for it cannot afford to question the person who nourishes it. Therefore, it has to completely deliver itself to the person. It is like an adult who delivers himself or herself to an anaesthesiologist. Looking at the anaesthesiologist, you do not even think that you can deliver yourself to this person, a mortal. First you have to sign up a paper where it is written that even if you do not come back alive, it is your responsibility. It is not that person's responsibility. You sign consciously before becoming unconscious.

Now coming back to the baby, it does not have the wherewithal to survive. As an organism it is programmed to survive; it has got that instinct. It is the only goal in the beginning. There is no other goal. Ask the baby, "What is the goal of life?" If it can answer, it will say, "I want to survive." It has no other goal. It is not going to say, "I want to become the president of this country," "I want to become the prime minister of this country," and so on. Survival is the organism's untold story. It is the story of every organism.

A CHILD'S TOTAL TRUST

The baby is helpless. It cannot even turn much less it has any resource to survive. It delivers itself to what I call trust. Do you know what kind of trust? It is total trust. You can have total trust only in someone who is all-knowledge and all-power. You cannot place absolute trust in a person who is fallible, bound by time, bound by ageing, bound by disease and death. You cannot totally trust that person who can create, but can create only small things, and who also says he cannot do anything else; much less can you trust a person who can create but cannot maintain what he creates. Perhaps a person can create, can keep it going, but cannot withdraw, cannot stop, like some people who do not know when to stop talking. Well, that person you cannot trust. One hundred percent trust is not possible. You can only trust the person who does not have any limitation whatsoever, as I have mentioned, in terms of knowledge, in terms of *śakti*, power. Whichever way you look at the person, he or she has to come up with a total capacity; that person alone you can totally trust.

However, innocence on the part of the child makes total trust possible. Total trust is very necessary for that baby. It cannot afford to distrust; it has got to trust. Therefore, total trust means that the trusted person nourishes, takes care. That person becomes Īśvara, God, for that child and on the lap of that person, it relaxes; it goes to sleep. To the voice of the person who rocks the cradle, or on the moving lap, the child goes to sleep because it is safe. In its awareness there is safety because of total trust. Safety comes from trust.

Gradual erosion of the child's total trust

A mother is trustworthy until her mobile rings. Once upon a time the door was knocked upon. Once upon a time the telephone rang. That was all once upon a time. Now the mobile rings and you are away from the child. The child feels deprived because there is inconsistency. You are not around all the time. I want you to understand this thoroughly. You cannot afford to be ignorant of a few things. You need to know.

Inconsistency causes disturbance to the child. In its awareness, the mother has to be around. As the baby grows, it also recognises the other familiar voice of a different frequency that was heard while it was pre-natal, sometimes in the morning and evening. Sometimes it is heard after ten days. Even that is a soothing experience and gives a sense of security. Well, this consistency on the part of a mother makes the child feel secure. She may not be a working mother. This 'working mother' is a new expression, as though the other mothers do not work. They work in the kitchen, go to the market; they work at home. As long as the mother is not away in the child's awareness, the child feels secure. As long as the mother does not fall ill, the child is secure. As long as the mother does not share the attention with another baby, the child is secure. As long as the mother does not raise her voice, the child is secure. As long as the mother does not argue with the other voice in a familiar frequency, the child is secure.

You can now understand that as the child grows, the insecurity also grows. It begins to see the fallibility, the inconsistency. Where is total trust? The total trust gets violated, gets eroded all the time.

In a joint family the child definitely had a lap, an empty lap. It sat on the empty lap of a grandmother or of an aunt. Now, there are no empty laps; even if a lap is empty, there is a laptop on it. Where is an empty lap? There is no empty lap available. The child grows insecure, remains insecure, constantly seeking the same safety, the same security that it had experienced before it was born.

This particular experience of the child remains all the time. It is called the unconscious. Every adult has the responsibility to process this insecurity with which one cannot live. To live intelligently, to live objectively, one has to understand this unconscious very thoroughly. The unconscious interprets everything. It vitiates every experience. It distorts everything. Nothing is seen as it is. We need to become conscious of this unconscious. We will.

Talk 2

Matured response is to understand the unconscious

In Sanskrit '*kaṣāya*' is an equivalent word for the unconscious. *Kaṣāya* controls our life; we have no control over it. The nature of *kaṣāya*, the unconscious, is such that we cannot have any say over it, inasmuch as it is something that we are not conscious of. Really speaking, our mechanical behaviour comes from this unconscious. Scriptures, such as the *Bhagavad Gītā* and the *Upaniṣads*, also address the problems caused by the unconscious. The word '*ātmavān*' of the scripture means the one who has *ātman*. Everybody has an *ātman*. *Ātman* here is the whole *kārya-karaṇa-saṅghāta*, the body-mind-sense complex. So, *ātmavān* is the one who has a say over the ways of one's mind. It reveals our *śāstra*'s recognition that one needs to address one's *kaṣāya*. In fact, the whole Hindu *saṁskṛti*, culture, recognises this as an issue to be addressed.

Unconscious controls one's life

Let us first understand this *kaṣāya*, the unconscious. The human child, the survivor, wants to have its Gods always on its side. Obviously it does not want to lose them or their grace. The child expects the parents to be totally free from any form of limitation. Where is the possibility? Knowledge-wise, power-wise, health-wise, longevity-wise, consistency-wise, the mother has to be free from limitation, but the fact is that the mother has limitations. As for the father, he has many more. Therefore, as the child grows, the total trust that it enjoyed gets violated. The helplessness of the child has not gone; it continues. The two-year-old is helpless. It has discovered its own ego, but begins to discover more and more limitations in the parents without verbalising them. The non-verbal recognition of the limitations that violates the trust is deadly. This is the pain that forms the unconscious. The child cannot afford to have this pain. It will die of pain. In nature, let us call it 'nature' for the time being, there is a provision for the child to put this pain under the carpet, the carpet of the conscious mind. It is the flip side of the ego, the shadow part of oneself, which we call the unconscious.

Impact of nursery schools on the child

In these days of competition, we send the children to school even before they are two years old. I saw in a nursery school, in Bhavnagar (Gujarat), a child of just eighteen months old. I asked for its mother but she was not there. The person who runs this school, and who happened to be my host, was very happy, joyous, that in her school there was a child of one and one half years. She said, "You know, Swamiji, this child is only eighteen months old." It was a complete and deadly violation of the child's trust. It was blatant. Already there are some violations that a parent cannot avoid. The mother has to go here and there; in between there are some quarrels, there is some headache, there is some shouting and so on. This is the mortal's lot which itself causes enough problems for the child. These are the normal problems of people. If a one and a half year old, a two-year old or a three-year old is sent to a school, separating it from the mother, it is a cause for neurosis.

In the child's awareness there is no presence of the mother. In fact, the child feels banished when it is sent to the school; the mother has vanished from its awareness. The child feels that the all-knowing, almighty mother, the trusted one, cannot commit a mistake. So, it concludes, "Something is wrong with me; that is why I am sent away." People say that this neurosis is a contribution of the society. The sociologists talk about this. It is all ignorance, nothing but sheer ignorance. The parents make this contribution. In fact, it is the mother's contribution. She has banished the child to the school.

The parents question, "How will they learn social etiquette, social skills?" What social skills? Do we not have social skills? Everybody has social skills. You can teach all about social skills in just two days; it does not take time. We need stable people. The parents also argue, "How will my child later compete in this competitive world if it does not go to nursery school? Further, these elementary schools will not give admission unless I have a nursery school certificate for the child." It is another problem. We need to change it.

These nursery schools destroy the stability, the sanity of the future generation. The current generation itself comes out of that. Later on, we push these children to score ninety-seven percent, ninety-eight percent, ninety-nine percent and so on, to get admission for higher studies. They have to score ninety-nine percent since ninety-eight and a half is the cut off mark; otherwise they have to pay a capitation fee. The father scored just sixty percent; the mother scored seventy two percent. If we go by the genetic average, the child should score only sixty six percent. How will he or she score that ninety-nine? Genetically it is illogical. Therefore, you constantly push the children until they have a break down. If they do not have a break down, you do not know what they will do later on.

Do not send the children to nursery school. You send the children to school from class one when the child is five years old. It is the correct thing to do.

Need for re-look at nursery schools

If one sends the child to a nursery school, then someone must accompany the child from home. Therefore, I say, let us have nursery schools where the mother also comes to the school.

"Swamiji, every mother cannot come."

"Then, why should she become a mother?"

"What Swamiji, she wants to be a mother."

"But then let her be a mother."

"No, she is a mother in the morning, a mother in the evening."

"What is she in between?"

"She is a working woman."

Even at the work place the feeling of a mother is always there. You cannot be a mother in the morning, a mother in the evening, and smother the mother in between. It is impossible. You are a mother always, even without the child. But if the child is without the mother, it is not right.

"All right Swamiji, but we need two pay packets; only then can we make both ends meet."

"All right, at least send the grandmother."

"When you say grandmother, you mean my mother-in-law?"

"Yes."

"That means she will stay with me?"

"Yes."

"Swamiji, that will be a big problem."

We have started two schools now in Chennai where mothers accompany the children. In fact, we should start such schools in every locality. Ask the children to come with their mothers and start one school. Do away with all the nursery schools once and for all or make them do what they ought to do. It is important that they do this because nobody has the right to destroy a life. All evidence says that it is not good for the child, for the whole society, for our culture, for our country. When someone goes against the evidence, then that person has not really understood. (Claps).

I appeal now to the sanity of the people. You need to be very gentle to your children, sensitive to their needs and never be responsible for separating a child from its mother, from its Gods. Never come in between a child and its Gods in the name of schooling. In our culture, you cannot come between a husband and his wife. You cannot even walk in between them when they are talking to each other. You cannot walk in between a mother and a child. You cannot walk in between a teacher and his student. You should never come in between the child and its Gods. This is very important.

Vedic system of education

In ancient times, we did not have this kind of a situation. When we read the *Chāndogyopaniṣad*, we find that Uddālaka, the father of Śvetaketu, sent Śvetaketu to a *gurukula* when he was twelve years old. We have to learn from the Veda. A child is sent to a *gurukula* only after it is twelve years old. Until then the child has to learn at home. It means that the teenage years are spent in the *gurukula*. It is a wonderful arrangement for the parents because they are free from the children's teenage problems. The teachers at the *gurukula* will take care of the teenage issues. Until the child is twelve years old, it has to remain with the parents and study. It is a very sane arrangement.

After all, Madam Montessori's system came within the last few years. We can change it again within a few years. Ms. Montessori was a good woman. She was right in this that the IQ of the human being can be increased only upto four years. Beyond that age it is constant. So her system of education was designed to improve the IQ of the child. She thought she was contributing something to the growth of the child. Little she knew that she was causing neurosis. This neurosis makes the child feel, "I am no good, that is why my mother sent me away." The worst thing is the mother telling me, "Swamiji, my child is different; she loves school. She comes back and tells me all about school and how she enjoyed it." More the child loves school, more the pain underneath. The child seems to be happy because it wants to win the mother back. Though the child expresses its great admiration for the parents, there is great pain underneath. The unconscious gets loaded day after day. By the age of four and a half the unconscious build-up is over, and then there is a conscious build-up. The conscious build-up confirms the unconscious, anyway. During one's entire life there is this feeling that 'nobody likes me, nobody wants me' and a sense of loneliness.

In this crowded *jagat,* there is loneliness. Think this over. When you look up, there are stars. When you look around, there are people and people. If there are no people, you have enough bugs at least. You do not lack company at any time. A person says, "Oh Swamiji, I am lonely. I am so lonely." Even as he says it the bugs bite him. How can the person be lonely? Nobody is lonely. It is only a sense. Since the child feels it is not understood, it thinks, "I have not done anything wrong. Why should I be sent away? Why should I be banished, punished like this? It is not my mistake; and yet, maybe there is a mistake because I am banished. At the same time, there is no mistake because I have not done anything wrong." Thus, the innocent child is really confused. The confusion remains during the entire lifetime of the person; it makes his or her reaction to every situation subjective instead of objective.

You project things that are not there. Simple things are converted into problems. For instance, somebody very dear to you was trying to sneeze, and that was exactly the time you asked the person, "Do you still like me?" The person was trying to sneeze and was making such contortions that his face looked as though he was frowning. Since his face looked 'frowning,' it was taken to be an answer, a negative answer. Even body language becomes a very big problem.

Need for communication at home

When there is no communication at home, people walk on eggshells. Parents tell me, "Swamiji, we never quarrel in the presence of our children." Do they really believe that the children do not know when they quarrel? Well, the children always sense that something has happened. Later, when the parents return laughing, the child sees something wrong in that extra laughter and walks on eggshells in the house. In the West, such a home is called dysfunctional. You can understand what a dysfunctional home is.

Structured society was a blessing

Long ago, the Indian mind was considered to be solid and secure because people lived in a highly structured and predictable society. If the father was a priest, the son also would be a priest. Therefore, there were no such worries as to 'what is going to happen.' The son would be a priest. He may be a better priest, more informed, highly educated and a scholar. So in the very profession itself excellence was accomplished. There was no competition. The son of a goldsmith was a goldsmith. The son of a carpenter was a carpenter. It was the only society where, for instance, a snake charmer came from a lineage of snake charmers; his father was a snake charmer, his great grandfather was a snake charmer. In fact his *gotra*, family lineage, is *paambaatti*.[1]

Snake charming per se is a bluff. No snake is charmed by anybody. The snake is deaf; it has no ears. There is no question of its dancing to the *punnāgavarāli rāga*, melody. The *rāga* is only for us. It is meant to put us to sleep, nothing else. How do you know? Let the snake charmer come and play the *rāga* with a flute. The snake will not get up; it will be sleeping inside the basket. The snake charmer has a special instrument made of a particular type of gourd that makes the snake mistake it for a mongoose and it wants to attack. The mongoose always wins, but no snake will give up without a fight. Therefore, it spreads its hood and keeps itself ready. When the snake charmer plays the melody, the instrument moves and the snake also moves. In fact, the snake is not dancing; the snake charmer's pipe-instrument is moving. This is the greatest bluff of the age, but it is fun. Let us not change it.

---

1 A snake charmer is called *paambaatti* in Tamil.

Similarly, the son of a *gudugudu-paandi*,[2] fortune-teller, being born in a family of fortune-tellers, would take to fortune telling as his profession and would marry the daughter of another fortune-teller. Therefore, there was zero competition in the society. Secure and structured, there was some sanity in the society. I do not want that kind of a social system to come back.I do not care for that, but I care for sanity and we cannot barter it away for anything. Why are we sacrificing emotional stability?

Happiness is accepting oneself totally as a person

A person is happy sitting under a tree. He does not have anything. This is something to tell the whole world. A person with a mere loincloth is blessed when he is happy and contented, *kaupīnavantaḥ khalu bhāgyavantaḥ*. It is not that all loin-clothed people are blessed, but there are people who are happy being what they are, even if they do not have anything. After all, what is it that you want to accomplish? You need to accept yourself as a person totally. If you have total acceptance inside and outside, you have made it. Until then you seek the approval of others, approval of the society. You want to prove yourself to be somebody. It is a constant struggle.

Stability in a structured society

We say this is a progressive society. Honestly speaking, India had a sanity that everyone admired. Even today, there

---

2 He comes with an instrument that makes the sound '*gudu, gudu*' and he is called *gudugudu-paandi* in Tamil.

is a reality that we better recognise. I do not say it as a credit to us. What is that reality? Every one of the post-war independent countries that became independent from the colonising countries, has had coups. Even in our neighbouring country, which was a country carved out of India, there have been coups, one after another; even now what is going on is a coup. Then, how come there is not a single coup in India? Is there something wrong with us? Did not India have situations where there should have been a revolution? Were there no occasions for a coup? There were occasions, but then a coup never took place. It is our culture; there is sanity and there is stability. I do not want to think that it is a left over of our past culture. It has not completely disappeared; it is still alive.

In a structured society there is stability. In a structured home there is stability. When the home is not structured, when what happens today and what will happen tomorrow are not very clear, the home becomes dysfunctional. The children are always in a panic.

Everyone has an unconscious which is why a lot of things happen to us, like *krodha*, anger. It is not that we are consciously getting angry. Anger is considered to be a *mahā-pāpmā*, the greatest enemy, sitting inside us. It is all *adhyātma*, pertaining to us. I am now addressing the *adhyātma*.

Anger is born of unconscious

At the level of desire, there is a certain choice involved. At the level of anger, the choice is surrendered. You cannot decide to be angry. You cannot consciously be angry even if I plead with you. I can ask you to clap, "Please clap." You can either clap, or you need not clap, because freedom is literally in your hands. When I said, "Clap, come on, clap," some of you clapped, some of you did not clap and thought, like typical Indians, "Others will clap, why should I clap?" In clapping there is complete freedom. It is centred on your will. You can either do it or you need not do it. Yet when I tell you, "Be angry for half a minute," it is a different request. Not being angry is one thing, but incapable of being angry is quite another. Not doing *adharma* is one thing, but being incapable of doing *adharma* is quite another. It is entirely a different level of your growth. Are you incapable of being angry just for half a minute?

"Swamiji, I do not say that we never get angry. But we cannot consciously be angry."

"Oh, you do get angry?"

"Yes, we get angry."

If someone says, "I do not get angry," I can very easily make him angry. A person said,

"Swamiji, in the past three years I did not get angry."

"Really? You do not look like that."

"No, no I never got angry for three years."

"I think you did not meet the right person or the right situation to get angry. For three years you escaped."

"No, Swamiji, I do not think I shall be angry any more."

"Are you sure?"

"Yes, Swamiji."

"I am not sure."

"Why Swamiji?"

"Because you do not look like that."

"What is wrong with my look?"

Here is the beginning of anger. I accepted that he would not get angry. You have to know when to quit; that is intelligent living. This is one instance. Well, one does get angry but not consciously, which amounts to saying that one gets angry unconsciously.

"Swamiji, it is not that unconsciously I get angry. There is always somebody who makes me angry." It is the unconscious. If somebody can make you angry, it is due to the unconscious. Nobody is capable of making you angry. You have given yourself to somebody in order for him or her to make you angry; this is the unconscious. It means that you live in a world of your own projection. There is no person or a thing in the world that can make you angry. Anger is a symptom. It is an outcome and an expression of pain that is there in the unconscious. The unconscious is a child frozen in time.

Everyone has a child in himself or herself. The child has something beautiful; it has innocence, it has freshness. It gives you those curious looks, asks curious questions, the what, why, how and so on. They always have the same freshness whether they come from the child outside, the child within or from the adult.

If the adult ego and the child are one and the same, integrated, then you always look at things afresh, always questions, always wants to know. You need that child, its freshness. Even now you have it. Yet when anger takes over, jealousy takes over, hatred takes over, you feel possessed.

Self-knowledge is the only saving grace to process the unconscious

Arjuna asked the question, "How come one does things even when one does not want to?"[3] It is an old question, nothing new. The reason for this is the unconscious, the inner child. Your life is controlled by the unconscious and you do not have any control over it. So the unconscious has to be ventilated, has to be brought out, has to be expressed. In life it keeps expressing itself; without your knowledge it happens. If you do not have an insight into this, it will continue to happen throughout your life. If you have knowledge, you can process the whole matter. If you have the space provided by knowledge, you can welcome your fears, your anxieties. Knowledge makes you can understand; it is the only saving grace. In modern psychology there is a branch that talks of cognitive approach. But our *śāstra* has been talking about this cognitive approach for a long time.

---

3 *atha kena prayuktoyaṁ pāpaṁ carati pūruṣaḥ. anicchannapi varṣṇeya balādiva niyojitaḥ?* (*Bhagavad Gītā* 3.36)

One-step response and two-step response

The inner space is provided by certain clarity and understanding of all that has happened to me. It gives me a beautiful frame of mind to also deal with others. Not only have things happened to me, things have happened to others too. A person behaves in a particular way because there is a background. I recognise the person's background in that behaviour. The recognition gives me the space; I will not immediately react to that person. This is what is called a two-step response to the world. A one-step response is, "How can you say that?" "How you can ever say that?" "How dare you say that?" It is a mechanical response.

With two-step response, you say, "Oh, there is a background behind the person's statement." You have the space inside to recognise there is a background for his or her statement; otherwise the statement would be unacceptable. It is unbecoming of the person. You understand that there is something behind the person's behaviour. This is two-step response.

A two-step response gives you the inner leisure, the inner space to deal with people of different backgrounds without being ruffled, without being taken for a ride. You can just step back and look at them kindly. Here is where kindness, compassion and understanding comes. If everyone has this two-step response then everybody is saintly. Saintliness lies just one step away. Everybody has this saintliness one step away.

You need to respond to your own issues; only then can you respond to the world consciously. You need to have the space to welcome your anger, your fear.

Managing anger

"Swamiji, this seems to be something different. We are always told to control our anger." If you control your anger, a few days later, you will have a *tsunami*. You cannot control anger but you can control the expression of anger. Please understand the difference. By not expressing your anger, you do not victimise your children, your spouse and others. Marriage does not mean having a sparring partner. You do not victimise anyone. 'Control your anger' is a loose statement because anger does not seek your permission to come. It does not ask, "May I come? I have been waiting for some time. May I come now?"

There is so much ignorance about anger that it has become a moneymaking issue, a moneymaking topic. At the workshops on 'how to control anger,' they say, "Whenever you are angry, think of this or of that. Divert yourself from anger." If you divert your anger you will develop 'diverticulitis'! Where will the anger go? You can only control the expression of your anger. You can use your will for this, that too with the help of people. Intelligent living is to seek help when you need help. If you can use your will with some help, you can avoid victimising anyone. This is called *dama*; *dama* means *bāhyendriya-nigrahaḥ*, control of the external organs.

You do not victimise anyone. But since anger is inside you, smoke will come out of your ears. To avoid that, you write the anger out. It means getting rid of your anger. You handle your own unconscious intelligently; you handle yourself intelligently. You cannot be ignorant about this.

When a New Year begins, you make a vow, "I am going to write a diary." Recently[4] you might have made one. Please check your diary; check all the diaries from 1999 onwards at least. You may have entries on the first three pages. The rest will be blank and it may have been used as a scrapbook. So do not make these unintelligent vows. Why do you make them? Be intelligent. You know that you are not going to write a diary, so, why do you make the vow? In the same way, never say, "Hereafter, I am not going to get angry." It is wrong. Instead, you say, "I welcome anger, but I will not victimise anyone. I will not victimise my children, my spouse, my in-laws, or anyone. I will not victimise myself either." It is clean as a whistle. It is not correct to victimise yourself. We need to handle this intelligently.

Welcome anger

You welcome anger. When it comes, you do not victimise anyone. It is easier with some help. You can help yourself and also ask your own family for help. You can convert a dysfunctional home into a functional one. Make it functional by telling everybody, "In this house, hereafter nobody is going

---

[4] This lecture-series was held in January 2005, at Chennai, India.

to victimise anyone because of his or her anger." It means when you are angry, you say, "I am angry now, I will talk to you later." Tell the others also, "When you are angry, say that you will talk later." Empower others also by saying, "Whenever I am angry, please remind me that I am angry." Tell this to your children and they will remind you before you get anywhere near anger. "Dad, you are somewhere near..." They know and they can remind you. They also learn not to victimise anyone. Make the home functional. You cannot hand over a better inheritance to your children than an honest home, a clean home where there is understanding. The growth, self-growth is in the home. What kind of a home is it where the self is crippled? What kind of a home is it where the children scamper to their own rooms or wherever they can hide themselves, because father is coming? The father's coming is like a warning, like a tiger's coming. Except the dog, everybody goes inside. There are some people from whom even the dogs go away. It is not right. This is not intelligent living. You need to be intelligent.

Subjectivity vitiates perception

You need to respond objectively to situations. It does take a step within yourself to respond objectively to a person or a situation. Your subjectivity vitiates your perception; distorts it. Sometimes the projections totally transform the situation beyond proportion.

Our *śāstra* recognised this distortion, this subjectivity as *adhyāsa*, a superimposition or projection. *Tasmin tad-buddiḥ* is knowledge. *Tasmin,* in an object; *tad buddiḥ,* a perception as it is. It means understanding an object as it is. This is knowledge. *Atasmin tad-buddiḥ* is the opposite of it, seeing on a locus something that is not there.

It is easy to correct an *adhyāsa* if an object is completely mistaken for some other object. However, the *adhyāsa* becomes very difficult to handle when the object is not totally mistaken for another object, but is seen with attributes that have nothing to do with that object. It becomes deadly in a relationship. Many a good relationship is broken because of this partial projection which is very difficult to remove. This projection, of course, is from your own unconscious.

There are two types of *adhyāsa, śobhana* and *aśobhana*. If you look upon an object as more valuable than it is, as though it is going to solve all the problems, it is called *śobhanādhyāsa*. When you take the object as something more threatening than it is, it is called *aśobhanādhyāsa*. Both impair your intelligent living.

Reducing your subjectivity

You need to relate to the world objectively. To be objective, you need to reduce your subjectivity. The problem is that you do not know how much subjectivity there is, how much *śobhanādhyāsa* or *aśobhanādhyāsa* there is. Here you need certain capacity to step back and look at situations with an understanding of how you relate to them, how you relate to the world. You know it very well, but at the same time you do not recognise it. Our problem is that we miss the obvious and go for what is not obvious. To relate, you must be present. The 'I' is the subject and what you relate to is the object. I am talking of the grammatical object. It may be a person, an object, or a situation. There is something that you objectify which you call object, and you are the subject who objectifies. The subject-object relating is living.

TALK 3

THE INDIVIDUAL AS RELATED TO THE TOTAL

You need to relate all the time to this world. In relating, the one who is invariable is the subject, referred by the first person singular 'I'. Objects are variable, whereas the subject is always invariable. The subject is always the hero. That hero, a he or she, is the central figure in all the situations.

TO BE OBJECTIVE IS TO UNDERSTAND THE SUBJECT

This subject is an affected subject. Naturally, the object is overwhelming. You are not overwhelmingly large and powerful. Small things like viruses and bacteria can take you for a ride. You cannot even see them; they are all the unseen enemies. Then the known, of course, are the big forces, the people. All these are there, and out to get you. The poor you is the affected you. Is there a sharing person? Is there anybody who can share your lot? If you seek someone to share your lot, the other person has his or her own load to share with you. You do not know who will console whom, who will help whom. The helper also needs help. Is it a losing game or is there any help within you?

THE INVARIABLE SUBJECT

When you look at this, one thing becomes obvious. Even though you are invariably present in all the situations, you see yourself as a complex being and not as one single person.

You are a son or daughter, son-in-law or a daughter-in-law, brother or sister, mother or father, wife or a husband and so on. There are so many entities in you and all these entities contribute to your problems. Upon this pile of problems is the invariable 'you' present in all these roles. 'You' seem to be the very soul of every entity, the soul of the son, father, husband, brother and so on. Therefore, the entity is only a status change relevant to the related person. You are there very much, but the status changes. If the status changes, then naturally, the problem of the son is only the problem of that role played by the person. The problem is not you, the person. The person seems to be free from the one that suffers the problem.

Roles of an actor and roles in real life

The roles that you play in your life are like the roles an actor plays on the stage. Let us suppose an actor plays the role of a begging person who undergoes a lot of privations, according to the script of the play. However, the actor does not seem to be affected by the role. In one situation he is supposed to cry aloud. He cries so well that he brings real tears from his eyes. He is happy within because he is crying so well. Later, after the scene is over, his friend who was sitting in the audience comes backstage to congratulate him. "Hey, that crying was marvellous. How did you do it? Did you have an onion peel? How did you bring out those real tears?" The actor is very happy that he could cry so well.

Why does he not play the roles in the same way in real life? Every status change is looked upon as a role. Son is a role, father is a role, husband is a role. All the roles are only referential; you are not the son, you are not the father, you are not the husband. When you look at yourself in relation to your parents, you are the son or the daughter. When you look at yourself in relation to your children, you become the father or the mother. It is relative.

In a theatre it is very easy to be aware of oneself while playing a role. There, one knows one is not a real king, in spite of all those gilded robes and the use of the first person plural 'we'. The whole thing is a drama. One knows one is the son of so and so who is playing the role of a king or son of somebody else.

Real life, however, is not seen as a drama. The person is affected. Everyone affects the person. If you look at each role this affected person plays, there is no role without a problem. Either in real life or in a play, there is no role without problems. Every role is fraught with problems. Very rarely, is there a role that is free from problems. In a play you know clearly that it is a role, the space between the role and the person is very evident. But where is this space in real life? You do not find any space; inside it is all crowded. As a son or daughter, you have some problems; as father or mother you have problems and all these problems are centred on you, the person. Where is the space that obtains when an actor plays a role in the theatre? The space is not physical.

The role is the person. The begging person B is A, the actor. When B comes out, actually A comes out. Really speaking, B does not come out. Therefore, B is A. When B is A, our simple algebra says that A is B. It is not so here, sir. Why?

In fact, A assumes the role of B without losing his identity. All through the play the actor remembers that he is so and so, even though, as an actor, he identifies with the role's emotions in keeping with the script. All the while he remembers himself, his riches while assuming the role of a begging person. There is space.

Space of self-awareness

What is that space? The problems of the role are confined to the role. They are not allowed to enter into, to affect, the person A, the actor, because, there is space, the space of self-identity, self-awareness. That space is unaffected. A, the actor, is *asaṅga*, untouched. A is very much present in B, the role of the beggar. Every bit of B is A. There is no B without A. The whole of B is the whole of A. But at the same time A remains uninvolved. It is very evident here. The space is very clear. Therefore, the person remains unaffected.

What happens in real life? The world keeps changing because it is variable. You are also variable, in the sense you assume a relevant change as the situation changes. If few people are standing in front of you, and the first person is your father, the second person is your mother; you become your father's son in front of your father and a mother's son in front of your mother. A father's son is different from a mother's son. Then the third one is a sister; you become the brother. It does not take time. The next is the spouse, then a friend and so on. Relevant to the person you relate, you change. This is called sanity.

Sanity is to bring out the right person for the situation. You cannot afford to bring out the wrong person. True. Yet while playing roles in real life, that space is not there for want of knowledge of the actor, the person. That you are different from the roles you play, is very obvious. You are an entity, a person, the meaning of the first person singular, *aham*, I. Away from the role, this I is a conscious being. This conscious being has to be understood. You have to correct all your wrong opinions about yourself and see clearly who you are in order to play the roles in real life as one does in the theatre.

Total is both known and unknown

It is not enough to say that I am a conscious being because I am also an individual with reference to this body-mind-sense complex. As an individual alone I am a conscious being. This conscious being is also related to the total. It is like a tree in a forest which is related to the mother tree, to its own brother tree and to the other small trees growing in the forest. While the tree is inter-related to other trees, at the same time, it is related to the forest as an entity. If the forest is an entity and if this particular tree is related to the forest, then the relationship of the tree to the forest is the same as every other tree's relationship to the forest. It is a relationship of the individual to the total. The total is the forest.

As an individual I am related to the whole, to the total. There is no gainsaying this. There is no individual without the total. The total has to be understood. Without understanding the total, if somebody says, 'I' is consciousness, *ānanda*, bliss," it will not work because that person is bypassing the reality that the individual is part of the total. You cannot bypass this reality. Neither can you bypass your psychological reality. You have to address it. The question is: what is the total?

The total is all that you see here. What you see and what you know is very little. Your concept of 'all' is itself very small. The 'all' should be taken as known and unknown. The known plus the unknown is the whole. The unknown includes what is partially known, what is wrongly known, and what exists but is not known.

Let us suppose that the total is a conscious being. As an individual, I am a conscious being. But how do I understand the total? People look upon all that is objectified as inert. Some of the theologies propose that God created them for our consumption. God created man in his own image; this is what man says. What about woman? In whose image was she created? God created man in his own image and the world was created for man's consumption. Afterwards we worry about the environment. This basic theological concept, that the world is meant for our consumption, is destructive. It means that everything other than man is to be consumed because man is made in the image of God; he has the right to consume all that he chooses. Except for a baby, every other creature gets into the soup, that which crawls, swims, flies or walks; nothing is left out. The primitive man did exactly the same thing and we continue to do so. Once, I was travelling in a plane and the person next to me had ordered a crab for his dinner. In the middle of his plate was a dead crab, while all around the dead crab was civilisation. This is our growth. I think we really need to understand the total properly.

Confusion is when the total is not understood

I am an individual conscious being. The total also is a conscious being. If it is the truth, then my not knowing the truth will definitely create much confusion. I cannot enjoy inner space because I do not know the reality of my basic relationship. The actor knows that he is an individual; he knows all about himself as an individual. He also knows that the individual is different from the role that he plays. Here, I am that individual. Bypassing that individual conscious being and all about the reality of that conscious being is not going to give me any kind of space or respite; therefore the problems keep piling up.

I am not acceptable to myself!

Every role has problems. There are no roles without problems. If all the problems of the roles are rolled into one, then I become the problem. In fact, I am the problem. However, I think that the world is the problem. No, I am the problem. To whom am I a problem? I am a problem to myself because I cannot stand myself. The greatest tragedy is that I cannot stand myself. If I am totally acceptable to myself, then it is easy for me to be compassionate, understanding. It is easy for me to be giving; there is total acceptability. Here, no positive thinking is going to help.

Positive thinking will not remove self non-acceptability

Positive thinking implies being totally oblivious to what you do not like to see. In America they have doughnuts which are like our *vadais*. The calories for the *vadais* are nothing when compared to the calories of their doughnuts. A doughnut is big and has a hole in the middle. A person, a positive thinker, eats seven doughnuts every day. However, he does not want to put on weight, and is very conscious about that. He does not have any guilt either; he is guilt-free because he is a positive thinker.

What is positive thinking here? In a doughnut there are two parts. One part is full of calories; the other part, the hole has zero calories. If you are a positive thinker, you will say that you have eaten only seven non-caloric doughnuts. If you are a negative thinker, after a bite, you will always worry that the calories will appear somewhere in your body. Positive thinking means that you eat seven doughnuts but count the non-caloric holes. This is not thinking. We are not interested in positive thinking or negative thinking; we are interested in thinking, just thinking.

There are lot of things that we have and many that we do not have. Yet there is a possibility of total acceptability if only we care to know this basic being, to know all about this basic conscious being. Therefore, the journey begins here, as a person who means business and who lives his or her life intelligently.

Talk 4

Everything is 'given'

To live intelligently is to cover all the realities that are about me, around me. When I look at the reality of what I face, one thing is obvious; everything is given to me. When I was born, my parentage was already given. I did not have a choice. My childhood was given. I did not have any choice. The scheme of things, the world is given. For my survival, oxygen and so on are all given. I need bio-energy and therefore food is given.

Food is vegetarian

There is only one source for food on this planet; there is no other source. Food is from plants. *Adyate iti annam,* that which is eaten by us is *anna*, food; and it is available outside. It has to be prepared by the outside world. What is that outside world? Our Veda says,[5] "From the vegetation comes food and from food is the human." It does not say that any other food is available. *Oṣadhī*s are plants and trees. They alone know how to prepare nutritive food from natural sources.

Food is vegetarian. There is no non-vegetarian food. That is why you first say vegetarian, and then put one negative particle 'non' for the non-vegetarian. I will emphatically tell

---

[5] *oṣadhībhyo 'nnam, annāt puruṣaḥ* (*Taittirīyopaniṣad* 2.1).

you that there is a non-vegetarian meal, but there is no non-vegetarian food. In fact vegetarian food is good for health. We have to be vegetarians. Meat is not good for anybody. Even if it were good for you, it is not good for the animals. If somebody asks you about proteins, you tell them, "Ask the elephant from where it gets all its proteins. Ask the horse, the camel, the rhino, from where they all get the necessary strength."

I must state this fact. In evolution I find, the deer which is a vegetarian seems to me more evolved because it has two jobs. It has to find its food and it has the responsibility of protecting itself from the predators, the carnivorous animals. To find food, it comes out of its protective cover. It has to find water; it goes to the water hole. The predator knows this and waits for its prey. This is the way of life in the wild.

What about human beings? They are much more evolved. Not only has he to take care of himself but also has to make sure that in the process of his survival he does not destroy anyone. If he wants to eat the cow, then let the cow not be domesticated. Let it be in the forest. Like a Tarzan, but without a knife, let him go to the forest and fight with the cow, the wild cow. If he gets the cow, let him eat it. The cow has got a chance to get him. Look at the tiger. It is fair. It does not come with a gun. It does not come with any slaughtering weapons. It uses its own teeth, its own stealth, speed, power and its own paws to get the prey. The prey has a fair chance to run away, whereas from the human being, it is impossible.

Therefore, we are unfair. Fairness is *dharma*. We call them dumb animals. They are not dumb, we are. They live their lives. We destroy them when we are expected to protect them.

Life lives upon life. People ask the question, "The egg plant also has life." "Yes, true. But it has no legs." Vegetables are unicellular and meant for food. Only trees and plants prepare food for you which is why the apple tree produces one thousand apples. One paddy seedling produces a lot of rice.

We have to make sure that we do not compromise the universal value structure. Therefore, our responsibility keeps increasing. A mature person has fewer options. He does not need options. Maturity is complete when one does not need options.

The food, the earth, air, water, atmosphere, other life forms and the contemporary society are given to us. The universe, our solar system, the various forces, the strong force, the weak force, the gravitational force, the electromagnetic force, well, all of them are given. The micro world is given. The macro world is given. In other words, matter, energy, all the laws, the means and ends, everything is given. Possibilities that can be realised are given. New phenomena appear. In nature, new things appear while old things disappear. A *tsunami* is always a possibility. It happens. Nature itself can bring certain realities into being which were possibilities before. With some bacterial intervention, something new can be created. Some changes can be brought about. Human beings are always capable of new hardware and new software, for which the resources are given; all the materials necessary are given.

The *buddhi,* intellect, is given. It is not that you came into the world and did not find yourself with a *buddhi,* and later acquired a *buddhi.* In fact, we have been trying to use our *buddhi,* occasionally at least. So, the *buddhi* is given. That you can explore and know is a possibility and it is given. You can emote. Emotion is an important reality and it is given. You can love, you can hate. You can neutralise your hatred. You can neutralise your jealousy. All these possibilities are given. There are wonderful words like *vaśī, ātmavān, yuktaḥ,* the one who is together, who is on the driver's seat of one's life, who manages one's life thoroughly. You have to make use of the possibilities. It is done through your own initiative.

Initiative for emotional growth

Certain things are natural. A baby will become an adult. The baby is born, *jāyate.* It exists, *asti. Asti* means it is alive. If alive, then *vardhate,* it grows. In time, it gains *vipariṇāma* which means it grows into an adult. It is not *pariṇāma,* modification, but *vipariṇāma.* You need not do anything. You will become an adult, a potential mother or a potential father without effort. The '*asti*' continues all the way. Yāska, the original dictionary writer, quotes in his Nirukta these six *bhāva-vikāra*s, changes. Yāska does not talk about marriage and other *saṁskāra*s. After *vipariṇāma* he talks about *apakṣaya,* decline. Slowly, decline takes place. Normally, while reading you hold the book at arm's length. When you find your hands are not long enough and you cannot stretch further then you go to an ophthalmologist. This is called *apakṣaya*. All these take place naturally. The *śāstra* recognises this. However, emotional growth is not natural. You have to take the initiative, although the possibility for growth is given.

Possibility of self-acceptence is 'given'

The possibility of total self-acceptability is there because self-acceptance is there for every animal. Every monkey is happy being a monkey. We say that we have evolved from the monkeys. Do not go and tell this to the monkeys. They will laugh at you. You do not find monkeys standing at the American Consulate early in the morning. Indian monkeys are happy being in India.

It is important to know that I am self-conscious, and therefore, self-judging. When I am judgemental and find that I am not acceptable in my judgement, how am I going to accept the world? Nevertheless, self-acceptance is a possibility and it takes place by my initiative. The initiative is cognitive. Just as addressing my unconscious is cognitive, this also is cognitive. It is at the religious level. I do not even call it spiritual; it is religious. At this level, the fact that the individual conscious being has its own reality, a connected reality, should not be bypassed. In this connected reality there is a degree of self-acceptance in the beginning, and everything else comes afterwards.

There is such a thing as a relative self-acceptance followed by total self-acceptance. First I have to get the relative self-acceptance. It lies in my initiative and does not happen naturally. Once I am at the wheel, I have to drive. That is, I have to use all that is given to reach my destination. Here too, I am given the faculty of knowing, faculty of judgement. The understanding may be inadequate and consequently the judgement often is wrong. I have to take the initiative to live intelligently and understand the basic person who is called upon to play different roles in life. I can enjoy playing all these roles if only I enjoy the inner space that is available to the conscious being when that being is known totally.

Talk 5

The 'giver' is manifest as the 'given'

Understanding that everything is given gives rise to a natural question, is there a giver? You cannot but ask this question because what is given is intelligently put together, like your own physical body. This argument is to be properly understood.

If you look at any organism, it is intelligently put together. The micro world, an atom, is intelligently put together. A macro organism like this body is intelligently put together, inasmuch as it consists of different organs, each with a unique function in the scheme. It is fine-tuned. It has its place.

Intelligently-put-together presupposes knowledge

Anything intelligently put-together presupposes knowledge, whether it is a man-made machine, a spider-made web, a honeybee-made honeycomb, a weaverbird-made nest or a physical body. The weaverbird can make the nest it does because it is adequately programmed. The whole scheme is intelligently put together. Hence we try to understand everything in this scheme. We have partially understood and we continue to understand. When the scientist goes about conducting research, he does not think that this is redundant or that is redundant. He tries to understand why this is there and why that is there. He assumes that there is a purpose for this and that.

Nothing can be intelligently put together without conceiving its outcome. Even in cooking you plan first. This planning is called *tapas*. What do you have? What can be done? What is the time available? Who is going to eat? All these have to be taken into account. When even cooking implies planning, visualisation, then *sṛṣṭi*, the creation, definitely presupposes *tapas*, visualisation; it is one way of saying it. There is a giver who visualises the creation. Who is he? Here we can help ourselves with some logic, the logic of extension.

Creator of everything is all-knowledge

If one has created something, it is assumed that one has the knowledge of that something. Without knowledge of that something one cannot create it. *Jnāna*, knowledge and *śakti*, skill, are necessary for *sṛṣṭi*. Even for an ordinary pot there is a pot-maker who has the knowledge and the skill of what he makes. We extend this to the world. The logic here would be to assimilate what the *śāstra* says. *Ghaṭa-kartā ghaṭajñaḥ*, the maker of the pot has the knowledge of the pot; it includes the skill also. Now you can extend this to *sarvasya kartā sarvajñaḥ*, the one who creates everything has all-knowledge. When we say *sarvasya kartā*, we are talking of all that is given here, what is known and not known to us. The one who has the knowledge of 'all' is called *sarvajña*, all-knowledge.

Where is this all-knowledge entity?

So far, it is understandable and easy. The difficulty comes only when the answer is sought for this question,

"Where is this *sarvajña*?" We do not find anyone who is *sarvajña*. Everybody's knowledge extends only up to the next question. You ask a knowledgeable person,

"What is this?"

"A flower."

"What flower?"

"Rose."

"What rose?"

"Red rose."

"Why is it red?"

Knowledge stops here. All our knowledge extends up to just one more question. Therefore, on this planet we do not find one who is all-knowledge. Everyone is an *alpajña*, one who knows just a little. That is why there are specialists. Your own body is apportioned to many medical specialists. There is a neurologist and there is a nephrologist. There is a dermatologist who takes care of the skin. His knowledge is skin deep. It is literally true. For the eyes alone, there are many specialists, an optometrist, an ophthalmologist and then a retinologist.

Concept of God in Heaven is Illogical

Some people on this planet gave this all-knowledge giver, a safe and distant place called heaven. It means you are giving him a location. Once you assign a location, you are localising the person and, naturally, the person must have a body of his own. Here is where many mistakes are committed.

As long as a person can answer a question, he answers. Where he cannot answer, he assumes an air.

"Who created this world?"

"God created the world."

"Where is this God?"

"He is in heaven."

"Who created heaven?"

"God created heaven."

"Where was he before he created heaven?"

"That is God's mystery."

This is an area where we do not think. It is a dead area. We are yet to complete our enquiry of 'What is God?' Without completing this enquiry, we cannot ask, 'Where is God?' So the question 'What is God' has to be persisted with. If we persist with the enquiry, we cannot but ask the question, "What is the material that this all-knowledge 'giver' made use of to make this world?"

Material of which the world is made

Some say that God created this entire world, including you, out of nothing. Out of nothing, only 'nothing' can be created. It is only out of something that something can come. What that something is, is a different enquiry altogether. There must be some 'X' material which is called *upādāna-kāraṇa*, the material cause. The maker, *sarvajña* and *sarvaśaktimān*, is the *nimitta-kāraṇa*, efficient cause.

The material cause cannot be independent of the maker. Here our *śāstra* is a blessing. We can see this blessing in our culture, our language, our attitude towards every phenomenon, towards the world, towards money, towards knowledge, towards everything. Our attitude is one of reverence and this wisdom always percolates into religion. Religion and wisdom are manifest in the various forms of our culture.

Maker and material are one

The maker and the material cannot be separate. Space and time are part of the *jagat*. Our ancients have been saying this clearly, repeatedly. Modern physics corroborates this fact. It has called the bluff of time and space being absolute. Such a concept is now obsolete. We cannot say that the material was lying in space or somewhere separated by space. Space itself is yet to come. There is no question of the maker and the material being different or separate. They are one and the same. From one standpoint we call him the material cause. From another standpoint we call him the all-knowledge maker.

The dream model

One's dream experience helps one know that the maker and material can abide in one locus. In sleep, one does not experience the *jagat*, much less one's individuality. There is a statement in the Veda:[6] "*andhaḥ anandho bhavati*, the blind

---

[6] ... *tad yadyapi idaṁ śarīram andhaṁ bhavati anandho bhavati* ... (*Chāndogyopaniṣad* 8.10.1)

person is no more blind." Can it be said better? The blind is no longer blind. In fact, when the blind and the one who has perfect vision sleep, both share the same experience of not seeing anything.

Now, the sleeper wakes up half way, that is, he is awake to his own mind. In that state he dreams, and as long as the dream continues, it is real to him. In the dream he may experience hunger; his experience of not having eaten for three days. He had been on a mountain expedition where he had fallen down and broken his leg. With nobody around, he had been lying there starving. The experience is real. If somebody is chasing him and he is running, it is real. Everything in the dream is real as long as the dream lasts.

One good thing is that you cannot create in the dream anything that you do not know. Can you? You cannot, because to dream of an object you have to think of the object. In order to think of the object you should know the object. It is only with your knowledge and skill that you create a world for yourself. You think of the sun and the sun comes along with space and time; that is the truth. This is creation. You have such power that you can create the sun, the earth, the trees, the sky, and people.

You are the maker of the dream world. You did not borrow the material for the dream world from anyone. You did not find it outside of yourself. You are indeed a conscious being, the maker and the material cause. Not only did you create the world, you also became the world.

In dream you create everything, space, time, sun and so on. In fact, you are space, you are time, you are the sun, the earth, the trees, the birds, and all the people. You also create a body for yourself. It is all you. It is your knowledge that is manifest in the form of the dream *jagat*. It is the truth. You know intimately the fact that the maker and the material cause are non-separate.

Just as in the dream you are the maker and the material, if there is an all-knowledge and all-powerful Īśvara, who is the maker of this *jagat*, that Īśvara is indeed the material cause for everything.

EVERYTHING IS A MANIFESTATION OF ĪŚVARA

When we look from the standpoint of the *jagat* being intelligently put together, we call the maker the efficient cause, who is all-knowledge, Īśvara. From the manifestation standpoint, from the all-pervasiveness standpoint, from the material cause standpoint, every phenomenon is Īśvara. The entire scheme of things, the sun, stars, galaxies, space, time, everything is a manifestation of Īśvara.

Talk 6

Īśvara as various orders in jagat

I said that the individual is a conscious being who plays different roles in daily life. One is a son or a daughter with reference to one's parents, a father or a mother with reference to one's children and so on. Who is this individual? He or she is basically related to the total. We call the total Nārayaṇa or Parameśvara.

You cannot bypass Īśvara

You have to establish this relationship by recognising the fact that as an individual conscious being you are related to the Lord, who is all-knowledge, who is manifest in the form of this *jagat*. Let us call this individual conscious being *bhakta*, a devotee. The one who recognises this relationship is a *bhakta*. In this self-identity lies the space we need in relating.

You cannot bypass Īśvara. People want to bypass Īśvara and understand Vedanta. It does not work. It has never worked and it will never work. In fact the equation is between *jīva*, the individual, and Īśvara, the total. When you recognise this relationship, you are a devotee first and a devotee last. Basically you are a devotee, because of your awareness of the reality of the total, Īśvara, who is manifest in the form of the *jagat* that includes your body, your mind and your senses. Total means your mind is also included.

So if you are a son, then you are a devotee son; if you are a father, you are a devotee father and so on. This is the reality.

Relating to Īśvara is not born of choice

Intelligent living implies recognising what is. I do not consider bringing in Īśvara is a choice. Do you have a choice in being a son or daughter? You are either a daughter or a son. You have a choice when you say, "I do not want to marry, I want to remain single." It is a choice. You cannot say, "I do not want to be a son or daughter," although you can say, "I do not want to be a son, I wish I were a daughter." You can wish for so many things. However, you have no choice here. You are a son; there is no choice whatsoever because it is the reality. Similarly, you have no choice in being a devotee.

You accept what is. What is, is Īśvara. What is this Īśvara, if you do not accept 'what is?' Without Īśvara the total, all that you have in life is only a pile up of problems as a father, as a son and so on. You have to play many roles and every role is fraught with problems. If you recognise you are basically a devotee, then you become a devotee father, a devotee son, a devotee brother, and so on. The devotee is the cushion, the space. This is what you require. The space is enjoyed by being a *bhakta*. This is pragmatism, religious pragmatism.

A bhakta sees everything as Īśvara's glories

To assert the entity of a *bhakta*, Lord Kṛṣṇa, in the *Bhagavad Gītā* devotes an entire chapter called *Vibhūti Yoga* wherein he says,[7] "Any thing or being you see that has some glory, fullness or that is powerful, know all of them to be a ray of my total glory." Any manifestation you see here is Īśvara's glory. I just want you to recognise this. Wherever there is a pair of eyes of a human being or of any being, whether blue eyes, brown eyes, black eyes, split eyes, eyes in an owl, eyes in a beetle or eyes in a crow, there is sight. Eyesight is a glory of Īśvara. Wherever there are ears, there is hearing. It is all Īśvara's glory. This is called *samaṣṭi*, total. *Samaṣṭi* means Īśvara.

To live your life intelligently, you have to recognise yourself basically as a devotee. As a devotee, you recognise the *vibhūti* of Īśvara in others' manifestations, in others' glories and in your own capacities.

When a human voice makes an unmodulated sound, what comes out is '*a*'. Therefore, the Lord Kṛṣṇa says,[8] "I am the basic sound '*a*' of all syllables and letters." Intelligent living implies our recognising what is. What is, is only Īśvara's glory. There is no personal glory.

Bhakta in you brings out the two-step response

The awareness that you are the *bhakta* does not often percolate to the role that you play in real life because the role and its problems are overwhelming; *bhakta* becomes just a name.

---

[7] *yadyad-vibhūtimat sattvaṁ śrīmadūrjitam eva vā tattad evāvagaccha tvaṁ mama tejoṁśa-sambhavam* (10.41).

[8] *akṣarāṇām akārosmi* (*Bhagavad Gītā* 10.33).

If Īśvara's glory is recognised in everything, it means that you see the entire *jagat*, including your parents and every person with whom you interact, as nothing but Īśvara's manifestation. It gives you space in your interactions. The person with whom you interact comes to you with his or her own background. When you appreciate that background, there is a two-step response on your part and it brings out the devotee in you, the conscious being. If there is a one-step response the devotee is eclipsed. Therefore, the two-step response is very important here.

APPRECIATING THE BACKGROUND

In two-step response you step back and look at the other person with his or her background. You need not know the person's entire background. There is no necessity for that. Unless you are a therapist, the other person is not going to talk about his or her background to you. Besides, no one knows his or her background thoroughly because the background lies buried in the unconscious. There is no one without a background and you need to know it. "Why did he behave like this?" "Why did she say this to me?" "Why is she not aware of those facts that I have already given?" "Why does she not respond to those facts?" "Why does he or she project so much upon me?" Well, all these exist because of the background.

If you recognise the existence of a background, then your response is not to what is being said or what is being done.

The response is to your own appreciation of the existence of the background. This knowledge makes you a compassionate person, a simple person. Compassion begins with you. Only then is compassion towards others possible. If you look at your behaviour as coming from one who has a background, then you can be kind to yourself. You welcome whatever comes and you manage. You manage your emotions.

Desire and anger produce *vega*, force. Why does the *Gītā* mention this force? It mentions because the *Gītā* recognises that *kāma*, desire, and *krodha*, anger, will not go but their *vega*, force, can be managed. The force released by desire and anger can be managed. It means that you do not come under the spell of desire; you do not come under the spell of anger. You are able to manage your anger. You need to manage your anger, as well as every other emotion. If you are able to appreciate the existence of your own background, then you can appreciate the existence of others' backgrounds. The two-step response is with reference to both you and others.

While the one-step response is born of *ajñāna*, ignorance, the the two-step response is born of intelligence, of self-consciousness that is born of Īśvara-consciousness. How? You bring Īśvara into your life because Īśvara exists. What exists, you come to appreciate. You recognise Īśvara in all critical areas. Recognition of the all-knowledge Īśvara is just not possible unless you are all-knowledge. How do you know what is all-knowledge? You do not know what is 'all'. Where is the question of your recognising all-knowledge?

Yet you can appreciate Īśvara. All that you require is to appreciate *samaṣṭi,* the total. Wherever there is individual glory there is *samaṣṭi.* If you confine yourself to your individual glory, you are living like the proverbial frog in a well. You can recognise the glory of *samaṣṭi* in the simple fact that wherever there are eyes, there is sight. You recognise this everywhere.

We can look at the *samaṣṭi* from the standpoint of an individual organ like the liver. In our *śāstra*, we do not have a *devatā*, deity, presiding over the liver, but we have *vaiśvānara*, the *devatā* presiding over the entire digestive system called '*samāna*' which includes the liver. Similarly, there are *devatā*s of other systems like *prāṇa*, respiration, *vyāna*, circulation, and so on. All organs and glands come under these systems.

Before eating, one does a ritualistic prayer. In this prayer, one says *prāṇāya svāhā* and offers food to the *devatā* of the respiratory system, *prāṇa.* In the same way food is offered ritually to the other *devatā*s. The prayer ends with *brahmaṇe svāhā*. *Brahmaṇe* means unto that Brahman manifesting in the form of physiological order, covering every living organism. *Svāhā* indicates an offering, an oblation. It is an offering of our *namaskāra*, salutation. Since things function, there is an order in the form of Īśvara. Wherever there is an organism, there is an order that makes the organism alive; unto that Īśvara in the form of that order, my *namaskāra*. In fact, our *śāstra* recognises Īśvara in this *prāṇa* form as *sutrātman*. Intelligent living is to recognise this order.

We can recognise Īśvara as so many orders. Things abide within certain order. Nobody transgresses the order without paying the price for it. For instance, if you touch fire, you get burnt. You cannot ask the fire, "Why did you burn?" If you ask there will be an answer.

"Did you burn my finger?"

"Yes."

"Why did you burn it?"

"I did not burn your finger."

"You told me you burnt my finger?"

"Yes, I burnt your finger."

"Then why did you burn it?"

"I did not burn your finger, I told you."

"You are blowing hot and cold."

"No, I always blow hot."

"But you give two answers."

"I did not burn your finger because I did not go after your finger."

"But you burnt it."

"You touched me and my job is to burn whatever touches me. If you touch me for a required period of time, I will burn."

It is order. It is how things function. We understand the laws that are there, the various means and ends and their connection. We understand the cause-effect relationship between things. We understand the connection between an action and its reaction. All of these fall under various orders.

A human voice alone can produce certain sounds. It looks as though people who speak a given language from childhood cannot be made to pronounce the words of other languages without certain accents, but everybody can be made to pronounce any letter in any language. If you know the human voice acoustics, you can produce any sound. We have such a map in Sanskrit. It points out from which part of the vocal apparatus each letter comes, and the type of effort required to produce that letter. All these are written down. This is the law. It is not anybody's creation. This is how the creation is. Consonants cannot be pronounced without the help of a vowel. The vowel should either precede or succeed it; you can say *ak*, you can say *ka*, you can say *ik*, and you can say *ki*. But just try and say *k*; you will find it is stuck in your throat. That is a consonant. What can be independently pronounced is a vowel. There is another vowel, a combined vowel, called a diphthong in English. The vowel '*a*' plus '*u*' is '*o*'. There are some people who pronounce '*om*' as '*aaauum*'. There is no *aaauum*; it is against Īśvara to pronounce *om* in this way. If you do, you are rubbing against the law. You have to go along with the way Īśvara manifests. This is intelligent living.

There is an order here. There is an *adhiṣṭhāna-devatā*, presiding deity, for every *akṣara*, syllable, for every *varṇa*, letter. Our sense of Īśvara, our appreciation of Īśvara is thorough. We do not say that there is one God. We say that there is only God. Therefore, we can have many *devatās*. When we look at Īśvara from any one *samaṣṭi* standpoint he becomes a *devatā*. We have to understand Īśvara as a total being, from the standpoint of the various things that are there in his manifestation. One Īśvara is manifest in different forms.

In physics we study Īśvara as the physical order. The physical order covers the entire universe. What we see is *adhibhūta*, a connection to the universe, and what we appreciate is *adhidaiva*, the deity behind the function. It is Īśvara's manifestation.

Further, we can understand Īśvara as the one who is manifest in various life forms, as the biological order. When we study biology, we are studying Īśvara. When we understand any principle, either in physics or in biology or in any other discipline of knowledge, there is certain joy. It is called *vidyānanda*, the joy of knowledge. In understanding, in knowing, we are in harmony with Īśvara, the all-knowledge, conscious being. With reference to that particular *vidyā*, we are free from ignorance. We do not look upon any *vidyā* as secular. Therefore, we cannot step on a book, be it physics or any other, without asking for its pardon. All *vidyā* is sacred. It is Īśvara. When you study medicine you are in touch with Īśvara as the physiological order. That is why we say the real *vaidya*, physician, is Lord Nārāyaṇa.

Assimilating the vision of Īśvara is not difficult, but it is not easy either. It has to be done intelligently. When you say '*idaṁ sarvam*' is Īśvara, the *sarvam* includes your body-mind-sense complex. Then, it is obvious that the vision has to include you as an individual. Īśvara has to pervade you, sustain you, in every way. For us, therefore, Īśvara is not an object of belief. Īśvara is not even an object of understanding because he is both the subject and the object. The vision of Īśvara pervades the subject; it pervades the object. It pervades as Īśvara does.

To incorporate this vision in our day-to-day life we need to reduce Īśvara to a general order, without resorting to reductionism. Since everything is Īśvara, the total vision is divided into many orders. Just as in a university we study different subjects, different disciplines, here too we divide our knowledge of Īśvara into varieties of orders, necessary for our assimilation. We cover the physical order, the biological order and the physiological order. It is one whole, one single vision assimilated in terms of orders.

A very critical order that we need to appreciate is the psychological order. Psychology is a modern subject. It is a growing subject, highly contended; different people have different ways of looking at the same problem. However, for us it is an adequately understood subject matter. We may not have all the big words such as mania, depression, schizophrenia and so on, but to live a healthy life, adequate understanding of the emotional being of a person is available for us.

Fifty percent of the *Bhagavad Gītā* deals with psychology. If we remove the psychological terms such as *rāga*, likes, *dveṣa*, dislikes, *kāma*, desire, *krodha*, anger, *mātsarya*, jealousy, *lobha*, greediness, *mānitva*, pride, *dambhitva*, vanity, and so on, the *Gītā* will be a small book.

Understanding the psychological order as Īśvara helps us appreciate a person's background and the outcome. When we appreciate the background, we appreciate the order that is psychological, the order that is Īśvara. Therefore, everybody is okay.

Welcome every emotion as Īśvara

You welcome an emotion, but you do not victimise others because of your emotion. You deal with your emotions. You recognise Īśvara in the form of psychological order, forming the background of every person including yourself. You can now recognise in every emotion your connection to Īśvara. When you do not appreciate Īśvara in the psychological order, it takes you away from Īśvara. In the *Bhagavad Gītā*, Lord Kṛṣṇa says, "Be one whose mind is in harmony with me."[9] Here, the mind means the emotions. This sentence of the *Gītā* can now be understood better. By understanding the psychological order you stay with Īśvara. Every emotion is the outcome of that order. No emotion

---

[9] *manmanā bhava* (9.34)

estranges you from Īśvara. Even the sense of estrangement is included in the order. It is also is in keeping with Īśvara's order.

If you are used to jealousy, hatefulness, a sense of abandonment, of loneliness, it is because you think they are normal. They are not normal, but they are expected. You can put all these in order; make them healthy and spiritually nourished. The moment you accept Īśvara, he blesses you in the form of the psychological order. When there is a particular emotion, you welcome it. The emotion becomes one of compassion.

Compassion is a very dynamic emotion. It is the emotion through which you see yourself as nourished by the hands of Īśvara. Now you can look at other living organisms, look at this entire world, through the window of compassion. You reach out and do what you can do. Love is the basic emotion which turns into compassion and dynamically helps you reach out to people. I do not think there is any emotion other than compassion that characterises a person who is highly mature.

One has to act compassionately

A mature person is a compassionate person, compassionate towards himself or herself. All that you need to do is to care for yourself. The truth is that you will not care for others unless you care for yourself. To discover compassion you have to act compassionately.

Suppose a person has hydrophobia and will not enter into any body of water. The appointed swimming coach is waiting for him to get into the water. The coach says, "Come on, get into the pool." The person argues with him.

> "How can I get into the water without knowing swimming? First you teach me to swim, then I will get into the water."
>
> "Unless you enter into the water, how will I teach you swimming?"
>
> "Unless I know swimming, how can I get into the water? I engaged you to teach me to swim so that I can get into the water. I have hydrophobia."

There is no other way. You have to make him get into the water. He gets into the shallow end and the coach says, "You swim now." The person argues,

> "How can I swim? I do not know swimming."
>
> "You do exactly what I do."
>
> "You are swimming."
>
> "Yes, you too can swim."
>
> "But I do not know swimming."
>
> "Come on, act exactly as though you are swimming."
>
> "As though swimming?"
>
> "Yes, act as though you know swimming. Act like me."
>
> "Oh! Then what will happen?"
>
> "Then you will learn swimming."

You act as though you know, you find yourself swimming. You fake it and make it. There is no other way. You learn swimming only by swimming. You learn cycling only by cycling. You learn driving by driving on the road with an 'L' board in the front, on the sides and at the back of the car. 'L' means leave me alone! You are the safest person on the road. They will leave you alone. You cannot sit in the garage and learn to drive.

So too, you grow by giving. In grabbing you get emotionally crippled. Īśvara goes far away. That Īśvara is recognised is not a wonder, but that you are able to keep yourself away from Īśvara, is a wonder. Really, it is a wonder. Nobody can keep oneself away from Īśvara. In compassion Īśvara is. You act to bring Īśvara into your life.

There are issues even without calling them psychological. These issues are unavoidable, because the child is born without a clue as to how to live its life, without any capacity to live on its own. Although the child has an instinct to survive, panic is unavoidable. The child will die if the panic is not kept away from its conscious mind. Īśvara, manifesting in the form of psychological order, keeps this panic, the pain and the fear, below the surface of the conscious mind to be processed later. It is meant for saving the child, but it is not meant to stay there forever. Unfortunately, it does and controls the child's as well as the adult's life, making one always a survivor. As long as the panic of the child, that is, its unconscious, remains unprocessed, un-addressed, it will control its life. Therefore, this *buddhi* has been given to us to take the initiative to address the unconscious. *Śāstra* is given. Our own capacity to think also is given. Our experiences help us to understand that there is something beneath the conscious.

Kṛṣṇa's validation of Arjuna's statement

You find Arjuna saying in the *Gītā*, "My mind is agitation."[10] He does not say the mind is agitated; he says agitation is the mind. Arjuna, who said this, was not an ordinary person. He was a hero, successful, ambidextrous, had acquired a lot of weapons and had fought with Lord Śiva for his *pāśupatāstra*, the invincible missile. Kṛṣṇa first validates it by saying, "It is true; it is very difficult to control the agitated mind."[11] This means that one has no say over the mind. Keeping the mind in one track is like catching the wind by the hand.

The psychological order, therefore, is another critical manifestation. Critical because one lives one's life here at the level of one's mind. Living is relating and relating comes from here; the response is from this level. It is not totally at the conscious level. It is sheer grace of Īśvara that there is unconscious, but one needs to recognise that it is meant only to save the child, not to persist. Otherwise one is mechanical. When one recognises that one is mechanical because one is controlled by the unconscious, then one is not mechanical. One is conscious. When one looks at it as a manifestation of

---

[10] *cañcalaṁ hi manaḥ kṛṣṇa* (*Bhagavad Gītā* 6.34).

[11] *asaṁśayaṁ mahābāho mano durnigrahaṁ calam* (*Bhagavad Gītā* 6.35).

Īśvara's order, then whatever happens to a person, is in order. This is not an ordinary thing.

Kālidāsa writes, "I salute Lord Śiva and Pārvatī who are the parents of the universe."[12] It is very interesting. He addresses the Lord as both father and mother. The phrase '*jagataḥ pitarau*' stands for the *nimitta-kāraṇa,* the intelligent cause, and the *upādāna-kāraṇa,* the material cause. These two causes can be called father and mother. Why should we invoke the Lord as father and mother? Why should we not? We can invoke the Lord as father and mother because they are the final causes whose manifestation is this *jagat* itself.

The mother-father concept is important because we looked upon our own mother and father as omniscient when we were children. Only then could we have had total trust. Total trust means the trusted person should be limitless, in whichever way we look at the person, in terms of limitless *jñāna,* knowledge; limitless *aiśvarya,* over-lordship; limitless *śrī,* wealth, and limitless *vīrya,* courage.

Search for the infallible

Total trust in our parents, however, is not possible since both father and mother are bound by time, place and their own limitations. Being mortals they cannot be limitless. Yet the child cannot survive without looking upon

---

[12] *jagataḥ pitarau vande pārvatī-parameśvarau* (*Raghuvaṁśa* 1.1).

them as totally trustworthy because it is totally helpless. So total helplessness is compensated by total trust. Therefore, the parents become an altar of total trust. The child, who is afraid of a cockroach, runs to the mother when it sees one; the mother sees the cockroach and screams. Then, the father does the needful and he becomes great. This is how a shift in trust takes place. The father is now omnipotent. He is almighty because he can deal with this cockroach, although he has his own problems. In the room there is a lizard, a gecko, because of which he cannot sleep. He asks the night watchman to chase it away; until then he stands outside. Any manner of inconsistency is a problem. So the child goes on discovering that its trust is violated.

The whole life, therefore, becomes a search for the infallible. When I have recognised Īśvara as one great order, in my awareness, in my understanding, Īśvara is infallible. In fact, infallible is Īśvara in the form of order. Being in the form of order, he is physically infallible, biologically infallible, physiologically infallible and psychologically infallible. What never fails is order. It is called order because it never fails. What about disorder? There is disorder only because there is order. Therefore, every disorder is available for understanding, including mental disorder.

In my awareness of Īśvara as the father and the mother, I have settled all accounts with my own father and mother. I can bring that awareness of Īśvara to see that I am in order.

ĪŚVARA THE GREATEST THERAPIST

When there is fear, I welcome it in so many words. When I welcome fear, I welcome Īśvara. I go one step backward. Fear is my immediate response to the world. It is not a conscious response; it is the unconscious. In the unconscious response, the frozen child is definitely there, controlling my response. Therefore to welcome fear, I take a step backward, make a two-step response, which means I welcome Īśvara. This is how Īśvara is; this is how the order is. Once I realise this, with reference to my own response, I become a healer to myself. I consciously become a therapist to myself. Actually Īśvara becomes the greatest therapist for me in the form of order, because the infallible is Īśvara.

A local therapist may say, "I am sorry, I did not understand what you said." He has to say that now and then. You talk to a therapist because there is nobody else available to talk to. You pay the therapist and talk to him. You talk very relevantly about what is to be talked about; you pour out everything because you have paid him. The payment is important and is part of the therapy. It is a particular way of getting out all that is within you. You ventilate your mind.

You help yourself with your awareness that the infallible is Īśvara. In the eyes of Īśvara you are totally validated. You cannot be otherwise. Īśvara will always smile and say, "This is how you would be according to the order that I am. It was expected." You cannot surprise Īśvara.

The infallibility of Īśvara gives you total validation. If you says God is infallible, then he can become fallible if he does not answer your prayers. When the *tsunami* comes you may question, "Why does God do these things?" In this universe, even if one planet like our earth moves out of its orbit and falls into the sun, it is not even equal to a fleabite on an elephant; nothing happens. The other day I read that one black hole has been swallowing many solar systems. A black hole forms when a star burns out and becomes dense matter, attracting everything to it. Even light cannot escape which is why it is called a black hole. Nothing happened when solar systems were disappearing into black holes.

In this vast universe, the vastness of which cannot even be imagined, any happening should be understood prayerfully. Awareness of Īśvara helps you address your unconscious and enables you to take charge of your life. The unconscious is your time-frozen child that controls your life. That is Īśvara's order. The conscious mind has to take care of the unconscious. The adult has to take care of the child. The child has to be integrated, allowed to express itself without victimising anyone outside. You embrace the child, the shadow of yourself. This is the psychological order that is Īśvara. Īśvara's infallibility always remains.

Dharma is only with reference to a human being

We have another order in the manifestation of Īśvara, the order of values, the order of *dharma*. We do not say *dharma* alone is Īśvara. We say *dharma* is another critical manifestation of Īśvara that is necessary for a human being to relate to the world. Relating to the world naturally has to conform to this part of Īśvara. Lord Kṛṣṇa says something very beautiful, "I am in the form of desire that is not opposed to *dharma*." [13]

It means that *dharma* is only for a human being. No animal has to be taught what is *dharma*. No monkey has to be told that it should not eat this or should not do that. Suppose a cow that goes to New York is given a hamburger. It will take this side of the bun and that side too. It will also take some lettuce or whatever. What is in between, it will leave for the humans.

All animals are completely released from the choice involved in *dharma* and *adharma*, whereas human beings have to be told to conform to *dharma*. A person may be a vegetarian for ages, born into a family of vegetarians who have been vegetarians for generations. Now, this person wants to make a choice. He has all those funny ideas about proteins, how to get them and so on.

One cannot rub against dharma to fulfil a desire

The animals, being programmed, live their lives as they are supposed to; their desires are inhibited. Human desires, on the other hand, are totally uninhibited. You can desire for

---

[13] *dharmāviruddho bhūteṣu kāmo'smi* (*Bhagavad Gītā* 7.11).

not only what you have seen, you can also desire for what you have heard about. You can desire heaven, paradise; the inhibition is gone. Īśvara is completely manifest in this *icchā-śakti*, capacity to desire.

Desire is within the order of Īśvara. It is the *śakti* of Īśvara and therefore in every human being the desire is Īśvara. When the Lord says, "I am in the form of desire," his *icchā-śakti* is manifest. It is total. When you have more ambitions, you have more Īśvara. Let desires be there.

Īśvara is in the form of desire and in the form of *dharma*. While fulfilling desires, you cannot rub against *dharma* because that too is Īśvara. Why should you be told to follow *dharma*? It is because you have the faculty of choice, you can freely desire. Freedom is given to you. You have a free will. In a vehicle you are given a programmed free wheel; you can go forward, backward, left, right, or you can stop. You can do all this. Whereas, the free will is given. Once free will is given, the responsibility is also given. The more evolved you are, more the responsibility you have.

Freedom of choice empowers one to make or mar

The capacity to make choices can empower you to use or abuse that choice. If freedom is not there, there is no choice. When there is freedom, there is choice and there is a chance for abuse. There is a tendency to abuse because inside there is fear, there is anxiety. Your anxieties, your jealousies, your insecurities, all come to fray. They condition the pursuits. Therefore, one goes for the convenient; one does not go for what is right all the time. When what is right is convenient, then there is no problem. Sometimes what is right is not convenient. In fact, more often than not, doing what is right is inconvenient, and doing what is wrong is convenient.

It is like walking diagonally on somebody's vacant corner plot. There is a board that warns, 'trespassers will be prosecuted.' You remove the board and walk. Only when the board is there you are trespassing. If you remove the board, there is no trespassing. People keep walking and soon create a footpath. Later they claim that they have been using the footpath for a long time, they must have the right of use and the owner cannot fence the land. It is modern India. It is not ancient India, not even India fifty years ago. You do something wrong and say that since you have been doing it for a long time, you should now be allowed to do it legitimately. This is *adharma*.

One is free from guilt when fulfilling a dharmic desire

Going against *dharma* is the tendency. You have to curb this tendency before fulfilling any desire. You can have more ambitions. Lord Kṛṣṇa says that you can fulfil your desire, but asks you to remember that he is also *dharma*. When you fulfil a desire in keeping with *dharma*, you are free from guilt. The *upaniṣad*s recognise this fact. This is maturity.

A mature person gains wisdom. Maturity lies only in this and in nothing else. Wisdom is not going to descend suddenly. You have to live in a mature way. You have to grow into a complete man, a complete woman. The completeness is in terms of your capacity to conform to *dharma* from the beginning. You grow and become so complete that you are incapable of going against *dharma*. First you deliberately make an attempt to conform to *dharma*. You pray to the Lord in the form of *dharma*, "Help me conform to *dharma*." You invoke his grace. It is not easy to conform to *dharma*, especially when everybody else follows *adharma* which is why when *adharma* is overwhelming, you pray for an *avatāra*, incarnation, to come so that you can follow *dharma*. You need to have Īśvara's grace to follow *dharma*. You invoke the same Īśvara in the form of *dharma*. Since *dharma* is a universal manifestation, it is an order.

Dharma is universal

What you do not want others do to you, others also expect the same from you. You do not want to be hurt, robbed, cheated, or deceived in any manner. You want others to be compassionate, to be giving and loving. This is *dharma*. That is why we call the 'act of giving' as *dharma*. In no other culture is giving called *dharma*. Others call it charity. Charity is the most uncharitable word because you assume a patronising attitude when you give charity.

We live a symbiotic life. We need each other; we need to help each other. Therefore, giving is *dharma*. It is a kind of duty.

We expect people to be giving. Definitely, we can be very understanding. We can be accommodative. We can understand others' limitations, as we need them to understand our limitations. This understanding is something very profound in our day-to-day life.

Adharma creates guilt

For us *dharma* is a manifestation of Īśvara and Īśvara is manifest in the form of laws. The laws govern everything. *Dharma* is one side of the manifestation. The other side of *dharma* is *karma*. When there is *dharma* there should be *karma*. One always complains, "Swamiji, this man has done so much *adharma* and he prospers, but I have been doing *dharma* and I am not progressing. The other person has so much money. I mean he receives money above the table, under the table, with his right hand and with his left hand."

It means all *karma*s of the person is going against *dharma*. When one does something that is against *dharma*, naturally that *karma* must have a *phala*, result; not only *dṛṣṭa- phala*, a visible result, but also *adṛṣṭa-phala*, an unseen result. The person, no doubt, has a lot of money, but also has the other *dṛṣṭa-phala*, guilt. He cannot do it without having guilt. Growth lies in asking, "How come I did not do the right thing? How come I did the wrong thing?" The Veda talks about this,[14] "Why did I not do the right thing? Why did I do the wrong thing?" Guilt is the worst thing that one can have.

[14] *kimahaṁ sādhu nākaravam. kimahaṁ pāpam akaravam iti* (*Taittirīyopaniṣad* 2.9)

A guilt-free life is living a complete life. This is *dṛṣṭa-phala*. *Pāpa-karma* accrued to a person will definitely manifest in the form of the most uncomfortable situations, either in this life or in some other life.

Going against dharma creates hurt

The law of *karma* is, only because there is *dharma*. Where there is *karma, karma-phala* will also be there. This is our *śāstra*. To live intelligently is to be aware of both *dharma* as well as *karma*. Desire has to be acted upon, if it needs to be fulfilled. When you act upon your desires, naturally, there is going to be an action in keeping with *dharma* or against *dharma*. The law is, when you rub against *dharma, dharma* rubs you. Find an old tamarind tree and with your bare back, rub the tree ten times. Then look at the tree. Nothing has happened to the tree. The tree is standing; if at all anything has happened, some dead bark has fallen. You rubbed the tree and the tree has rubbed you quietly, without doing anything, standing where it was. After that, for days you cannot wear a shirt because your back is bruised. You rubbed the tree and the tree rubbed you. It is the law. When you rub, you are the one to rub and also get rubbed; it is law. Action and reaction are both equal and opposite. It is Īśvara's law.

You cannot rub against *dharma* without getting rubbed in the process. It is law of *karma*. To live intelligently is to be aware of all this. Take responsibility not only for your life, but also for your fellow beings. Fulfil the needs of the society wherever the society needs something that you can offer.

You do what you can. You cannot say, 'let others do it.' It starts with you. You begin doing what needs to be done, and when you begin doing that, change takes place.

YOU MAY BE THE HUNDREDTH MONKEY!

There is a story in a small booklet titled '*You may be the hundredth monkey.*' There were some monkeys living in an island. Once, there was a big drought. There was no food and the monkeys were starving. One day, a monkey pulled out a root. It washed it in the seawater and began eating it. Another monkey watched this and repeated it. Then another monkey did the same thing. Soon, a hundred monkeys were washing and eating the roots. When the hundredth monkey ate a root, the monkeys on another island began doing the same thing. Therefore, the book is titled, '*You may be the hundredth monkey.*' The hundredth monkey brought about a change. We can make things happen. We do not wait for things to happen. That is how we bring in changes. We need to make things happen.

ĪŚVARA THE COGNITIVE ORDER

When we absorb the vision of Īśvara in terms of various orders, we include one more order. To understand the various orders, there is an epistemological order, which is manifest in all of us in the form of the power of knowing, the means of knowing. Our sense organs, backed by rational thinking, constitute what we call *pramāṇa,* a means of knowledge.

Not only the senses and rational thought are *pramāṇas*; we have the *śāstra* as one more *pramāṇa*. All these are, again, not separate from Īśvara.

The Indian villager has an attitude towards the earth; he does not look upon it as merely land, soil or dirt. He looks upon it as *bhūmidevi*. In the vision of the villager Īśvara is not in one place having a location. If his vision is not damaged by any external influence, he or she still feels that Īśvara is everywhere. It is reflected in his or her life in various forms.

Talk 7

Attitudes born of the vision: Īśvara is everything

In our culture the vision that everything is Īśvara has percolated into the cultural forms. It is there in our language, in all our forms of worship and in our attitudes. For instance, you can create an altar by just taking a spoonful of turmeric powder mixed with a little water and making a lump out of it. You invoke Īśvara in that lump by saying,[15] "In this form I invoke Mahāgaṇapati." In what is merely a turmeric powder, you invoke the Lord as the remover of all obstacles. Since he is the one who also creates obstacles as the giver of the fruits of your actions, you neutralise those obstacles by this *karma*. You have the capacity to invoke Īśvara in that turmeric powder. After the *pūjā* you release the turmeric powder back to its original state. Even though you have released it, your attitude towards it is not merely the attitude you have towards turmeric powder. It is a *mahāgaṇapati* attitude. Your attitude has changed. You cannot use the powder for cooking anymore.

Attitude towards money

All your problems are due to improper attitudes. An attitude is not something that you can create. Attitude grows

---

[15] *asmin bimbe mahāgaṇapatim āvāhayāmi.*

upon you. In our culture money is looked upon as not merely money, but as Goddess Lakṣmī; it is an attitude. This attitude is manifest all over India. Nobody will step on it. No Indian will step on money which is looked upon as Lakṣmī, a *śakti* of Īśvara. This is an intelligent way of relating to money. You need not cultivate this attitude; it grows upon you just living in this culture. Money is looked upon as sacred not because it has buying power. Buying power is not sacred; money is. In other cultures, money is not looked upon as sacred.

In Indian culture, there is only one vision that has percolated, the vision that everything is Īśvara. We do not give a location to Īśvara. We say that all that is here is Īśvara; every location is Īśvara. Space and time are located in Īśvara. In fact, space is Īśvara; time is Īśvara. The *upaniṣad* says,[16] '*kaṁ brahma, khaṁ brahma,*' *kam* means well-being; *kham* means space. So, all that is here is Brahman. We can now understand why wealth is a power. Money is a *vibhūti*, glory; that *vibhūti* is Īśvara. Sarasvatī also is Īśvara, which is why we do not step on a book. It is an attitude This attitude has grown upon us. It is a blessing and we need to realise its extraordinary value.

Attitude towards knowledge

Our attitude towards knowledge is the same. We do not have this division of secular knowledge and sacred knowledge. The *Muṇḍakopaniṣad* says,[17] "One must gather two

---

[16] *prāṇo brahma kaṁ brahma khaṁ brahmeti* (*Chāndogyopaniṣad* 4.10.4).

[17] *dve vidye veditavye, parā caiva aparā ca* (*Muṇḍakopaniṣad* 1.1.4).

types of knowledge. One is *aparā vidyā* and the other is *parā vidyā*." What is *aparā vidyā*? *Ṛgveda, Yajurveda, Sāmaveda, Atharvaveda, Śikṣā*, phonetics, *vyākaraṇa*, grammar and so on. All disciplines of knowledge, including microbiology, are *aparā vidyā*.

What is *parā vidyā*? That by which you understand Īśvara, the Lord, is *parā vidyā*. It is sacred knowledge. Then what about *Ṛgveda*? Sacred. What about *Yajurveda*? Sacred. In fact both *parā vidyā* and *aparā vidyā* are sacred. Knowledge is sacred because it belongs to Īśvara, the *sarvajña*. The *sarvajñatva*, the all-knowingness, includes all disciplines of knowledge.

Knowledge is not something which is gathered. It already exists in your consciousness. What inhibits knowledge is your ignorance. Therefore, the removal of ignorance alone is knowledge. It is an entirely different attitude. If you say the removal of ignorance is knowledge, then you cannot say that somebody is incapable of knowing. Every teacher scrapes off ignorance. If removal of ignorance is indeed knowledge then who is not capable of knowing? You also cannot say that a given teacher is not able to scrape away ignorance because various methods of teaching are there. If one method does not work, then another method works. For instance, you see an old pot and in one corner of it you see the brass. You just wash it, nothing happens. You put some tamarind on it, nothing happens. Then what do you do? You bring a special polish such as Brasso. You do not give up because you know that it is a brass pot. The shine is already there and what needs to be done is to bring it out. The patina that covers the shine has to be removed. This is knowledge.

The difficulty with the teacher is that he is working with minds. When you work with minds, you have to make sure the minds are with you. In teaching you have a double responsibility. One is to make sure that you convey what should be conveyed, and the other is to make sure that the mind of the person to whom it is conveyed is there with you. It is creativity and it is not that easy. I am talking of the attitude towards knowledge itself.

We need to assimilate attitudes

It is unintelligent not to understand the profound meaning of these attitudes. The attitudes remain with you. Some are very vague attitudes, unassimilated attitudes. Unassimilated attitudes really do not give you any self-esteem, self-respect.

I heard someone say that culture is the route to roots. It is a nice idea. You are your forms. From where do the forms come? *Namaste* is a form. Your *raṅgoli* is a form. Your *kuṅkuma* and *candana* are forms. Behind the forms there must be some meaning. If you do not know the meaning, and you have only forms, what kind of self-esteem can you have? You have to know all about yourself. To enjoy self-esteem you should mean whatever you do, especially in terms of culture and religion. The core person is a religious person which why a human being can be made into a bomb; he or she can be conditioned, indoctrinated. Unless you love and understand this core person, the religious person, you can turn into a bomb.

Form and spirit

In whichever way you look, there is meaning in all forms. Without assimilating the spirit of it, a form is like a carcass; a spirit without a form is a ghost. You do not need either of them. You need forms with the spirit. If someone tells you that idol worship is bad, that person either is refusing to understand or is incapable of understanding. Nobody worships an idol. You worship only Īśvara. Those who do not have the ritual of worship lose out a lot, because all that is here is a manifestation of Īśvara in the form of 'forms'. In fact, these forms alone constitute the truth of *vyavahāra*, transactions, in daily life. In what is empirically true, there is nothing but forms. They are manifestations of Īśvara which is why you can invoke in any one form, the whole Īśvara, or a given *devatā*. You need not be apologetic when somebody criticises you for being an idol worshipper.

In the North, an organisation came into being that said, 'We do not follow forms of worship, altars of worship.' This is wrong and it is not true. When you say prayers, words are but forms. A direction is a form. When you kneel down, it is a form. When you congratulate a person, it is a form.

When you shake the person's hands, it is a form. A birthday greeting is a form. The whole life is lived by forms. There is nothing but forms. Form is to be viewed, visualised, understood and assimilated by you as Īśvara. '*Īśāvāsyam,*' is a very beautiful expression envisioning the whole *jagat* as Īśvara. All that is here is nothing but *nāma-rūpa,* name and form.

Our attitude towards every form of expression is to be assimilated. We have now an attitude that grows upon us to assimilate the spirit of every form of expression.

Everything is sacred

There is nothing secular in our country, in our culture. Money is Lakṣmī because all wealth is a form of Śrī. Home is Lakṣmī, Gṛha Lakṣmī. Success is Jaya Lakṣmī. A child is Santāna Lakṣmī. It is Lakṣmī's or Īśvara's *prasāda,* gift, which is why we give the name '*prasāda*' to a child such as Gauriprasad, Sivaprasad, Rajendraprasad and so on. Who is not a gift, *prasāda*? Everyone is a gift, not by a person, but a gift by Īśvara; only then a gift is a *prasāda.* That it comes from Īśvara's grace is an attitude. *Karma-phala,* results of action, is also *prasāda.*

In life, we seek what is worthwhile and that is sacred for us. Knowledge is sacred, as is money. Vāyu, the air is sacred. Whether it is a bug or a plant, a tree or an animal, *Vāyu* sustains them all. '*Tvameva pratyakṣaṁ brahmāsi, vāyo,* you are

Īśvara, who sustains.' This is our attitude. Varuṇa, water, is sacred; *agni*, fire, is sacred; *pṛthvī*, earth, is sacred; *ākāśa*, space is sacred. *Liṅga* in Chidambaram is *ākāśa*. The famous *Cidambara-rahasya* is nothing but the worship of space.

Meaning of liṅgam

You need to understand what a *liṅga* is. *Liṅga* means that by which you understand.[18] In Indian logic, *liṅga* is a major term. The smoke would be the *liṅga* for inferentially arriving at fire. You do not see fire, but you see smoke and you say that there is fire. How do you say that there is fire without seeing it? It is because you see the smoke. What is the rationale? Wherever there is smoke there must be fire. So smoke becomes *liṅga*, a *hetu*, cause. If the whole universe is one single form of all the names and forms put together, then it would be a *liṅga*, a formless form.

Ākāśa is a *liṅga*. Īśvara is invoked as space. In Kalahasti Īśvara is invoked as Vāyu. There is, in the main shrine, a lamp whose flame goes on fluttering; fluttering because there is a hole somewhere and sufficient air comes to make it flutter. Vāyu is the inferred *liṅga*. In Tiruvannamalai Agni is the *liṅga*. Water is the *liṅga* in Tiruvanaikkaval. In Kanchipuram Ekambaresvara temple, the very earth is the *liṅga*, *svayambhu-liṅga*. You need to know all this because you worship them. All the five elements are, therefore, sacred.

---

[18] *liṅgyate anena iti liṅgam.*

THERE IS NO OWNERSHIP

Your own body is sacred for you. This body, made of the five elements, is given to you. The ownership does not belong to you, anyway. If at all there is an owner, the mother can make that claim. If the mother claims ownership, then the father can claim fifty percent. Being married, the wife can claim ownership of her husband's body. The children can claim, and the State can claim it too. An Indian body means amoebas have been living there for generations. They have an inherited claim. The sun, air, water, the elements, all can claim your body. Except you, everybody has a claim over 'your' body.

Suppose a judge says, "I am appointing a managing trustee; who is ready to manage this body? The one who manages the body should know the headache whenever there is one; should know the stomach pain whenever it comes, should know hunger and thirst, should know the back pain whenever it occurs. He or she alone, can manage this body. Therefore, who is ready?" The amoebas are silent, because they do not know how to manage. They only know how to destroy. They are all parasites and you are the host. They keep quiet. Everybody else also is silent. Nobody wants to maintain this body; nobody has the knowledge. Only one person is capable of running the show; that is you. You are appointed as the managing trustee of this body. You are not the owner of the body. Here, there is no ownership; there is only possession. Similarly, you do not own money; you only happen to possess it. You seem to have some right over it; it is just a legal device. It is like the flat that a person owns on the fourth floor of a high-rise building. He thinks that he is the owner of the flat. I ask him, "Who owns the land?"

"Nobody owns the land."

"How can you own a house without owning the land?"

"Do not ask questions. I own the flat."

"Then what is it that you own in the flat? The floor?"

"Yes, the floor is mine."

"But the floor is the ceiling of the person down below."

"That is true. The other day my wife was pounding something when the person from the third floor came up and kicked up a row, 'Is this your ancestral property?' So this floor is not really mine; it is the ceiling of the person down below."

"Then is the ceiling yours?"

"Yes, the ceiling is mine."

"But the ceiling is the floor of the person above."

"That is true."

"So, the left wall is the right wall of your left neighbour; and the right wall is the left wall of your right neighbour."

"That is true."

"Then, what is it that you own?"

If you live your life intelligently, you appreciate that you do not own a single thing in this world. You are only a managing trustee. Even if you have money, you can eat only for one stomach. Therefore, be a good managing trustee. If someone has money to manage then he or she has to manage it. Bhagavān has given it because of some good *karma*. You cannot say, "I cannot manage my estate." You have to manage and manage well. If you know that you are not the owner, you will manage well. You are the managing trustee of this body and everything else.

Intelligent parenting

You need to be intelligent in bringing up your children and in your relationship with them. Children are only born of you; they are not a part of you. We all think that they are a part of us. Each child is born of you, no doubt. It is something like a candle, lighted from another candle. It has the same power. The only difference is when the child is born, it is a baby. It has to grow as a whole. It is not born without a head or a liver. All the minute organs are there and as a whole it grows. Therefore, the child is given to you; it is *bhagavat-prasāda*, the Lord's gift. You are playing the role of Īśvara. That is why everybody wants to have a child; it is because the parents, like Īśvara, play the role of a creator. Really speaking, you are a *nimitta*, an instrument, in the hands of Parameśvara. Therefore, the child is a *prasāda*, a gift given to you and not a part of you.

Your hand is a part of you. You want to raise your hand, you raise it. Whereas, what happens if you ask your child to chant '*śāntākāram...*' when the Swami comes to your house? "Come, chant *śāntākāram...*" "Uuuuuum." Why? It is because the child is only born of you and not a part of you. When you ask the child to keep quiet, it will be chanting.

You complain when the child is a teenager. A teenager always thinks that he or she has got solutions for all problems. This is how we all thought. So it is a question of just enjoying them with great love; give quality time to the child. You have to bring up the child intelligently. Intelligent living implies intelligent relating. The child should know that its parents care. Then even judicious chiding is accepted. It is also a part of caring. When the parent looks into the eyes of the child, applause is there, congratulation is there, approbation is there, acceptance is there, admiration is there and approval is there.

Here was the mistake committed by Dhṛtarāṣṭra. Gāndhāri said, "I am going to blindfold myself, because my lord cannot see. What my lord does not see, I do not want to see." Dhṛtarāṣṭra went along with her without insisting that she be his eyes. Because of this their children did not have the parental approval, looking into their eyes.

Intelligent parenting is looking into the eyes of the child with approval. Otherwise, the whole lifetime that person will put his or her head down and talk. He becomes shy and cannot look into the eyes of people. Other problems, like seeking approval and so on, will also be there. Therefore, looking into the child's eyes is part of bringing up the child with self-esteem. If the mother does not have the time to look into the eyes of the child, like Gāndhāri who had blindfolded herself, you will get a crop of Duryodhanas. It is just an irresponsible contribution to the society. This was how the entire Kuru family got destroyed. Thanks to Kṛṣṇa one Parīkṣit was saved. Everybody was destroyed, all because of blindfolding. So bringing up children as *prasāda* is an attitude.

Body is a shrine

Your body is a shrine because it is a gift, *prasāda* given to you. The Lord is within and is a conscious being, while everything else is an object of consciousness. So you invoke the Lord in yourself. You need to assimilate this. You must have heard this when a *pūjā* is performed. A temporary altar is made and the priests ask you to go round the altar, and chant,[19] "Whatever *pāpas* that were committed in all my lives, may they be destroyed with every step of circumambulation." It is a profound *mantra* which means all your *pāpas* are destroyed as you go around. This is the prayer. If the room is very small and there is not enough space, you turn around yourself three times. What does it mean? It means the one who is seated in your heart is Bhagavān. You do not have a problem of self-esteem. This shows an understanding.

It is your attitude that makes your daily bath a *snāna*, bath to the Lord. Your clothes are *vastra*, clothing, for the Lord. Ornaments are *alaṅkāra* for the Lord. *Candana, kuṅkuma* and *puṣpa* are offerings to the Lord. It is part of your daily ritual.

---

[19] *yāni kāni ca pāpāni janmāntara-kṛtāni ca tāni tāni vinaśyanti pradakṣiṇa-pade pade.*

This attitude is born of your understanding, all that is here is Īśvara. Īśvara does not start from the unknown. It starts from you, the knower. This recognition will make you understand all your forms, all your attitudes.

I repeat, all that is here is Īśvara. This awareness makes me live an intelligent, pragmatic life, because I cannot estrange myself from Īśvara. I am not an orphan. There are no orphans and there is no orphanage. Only when I have no Īśvara in my life am I an orphan. Īśvara is for everybody. I have this attitude of being connected to Īśvara all through. This is intelligent living. I do not bring Īśvara into my life; I find Īśvara is already there in my life. All that is necessary is to be aware of Īśvara's presence.

Oṁ tat sat

Books by Swami Dayananda Saraswati

Public Talk Series :

1. Living Intelligently
2. Need for Cognitive Change
3. Discovering Love
4. Successful Living
5. The Value of Values
6. Vedic View and Way of Life

Upaniṣad Series :

7. Muṇḍakopaniṣad
8. Kenopaniṣad

Moments with Oneself Series :

9. Freedom from Helplessness
10. Living versus Getting On
11. Insights
12. Action and Reaction
13. The Fundamental Problem
14. Problem is You, Solution is You
15. Purpose of Prayer
16. Vedanta 24x7
17. Freedom
18. Crisis Management
19. Surrender and Freedom
20. The Need for Personal Reorganisation
21. Freedom in Relationship
22. Stress-free Living

Text Translation Series :

23. Śrīmad Bhagavad Gītā

    (Text with roman transliteration and English translation)

Stotra Series :

24. Dipārādhanā
25. Prayer Guide

    (With explanations of several Mantras, Stotras, Kirtans and Religious Festivals)

Bhagavad Gītā Series :

26. Bhagavad Gītā Home Study Program Vol 1-4 (Hardbound)
27. Bhagavad Gītā Home Study Program Vol 1-4 (Softbound)

Meditation Series :

28. Morning Meditation-prayers

Essays :

29. Do all Religions have the same goal?
30. Conversion is Violence
31. Gurupūrṇimā
32. Dānam
33. Japa
34. Can We?
35. **Teaching Tradition of Advaita Vedanta**

Exploring Vedanta Series : (*vākyavicāra*)

36. śraddhā bhakti dhyāna yogād avaihi ātmānaṁ ced vijānīyāt

BOOKS BY SMT. SHEELA BALAJI

37. Salutations to Rudra
(based on the exposition of Śrī Rudram by Swami Dayananda Saraswati)
38. Without a Second

Also available at :

ARSHA VIDYA RESEARCH AND PUBLICATION TRUST
32/4 Sir Desika Road
Mylapore Chennai 600 004
Telefax : 044 - 2499 7131
Email : avrandpc@gmail.com

ARSHA VIDYA GURUKULAM
Anaikatti P.O.
Coimbatore 641 108
Ph : 0422 - 2657001
Fax : 0422 - 2657002
Email : office@arshavidya.in

ARSHA VIDYA GURUKULAM
P.O.Box 1059. Pennsylvania
PA 18353, USA.
Ph : 001-570-992-2339
Email : avp@epix.net

SWAMI DAYANANDA ASHRAM
Purani Jhadi, P.B. No. 30
Rishikesh, Uttaranchal 249 201
Telefax : 0135-2430769
Email : ashrambookstore@yahoo.com

AND IN ALL THE LEADING BOOK STORES, INDIA